LIVING WITH THE ENEMY

LIVING WITH THE ENEMY

An outline of the German Occupation of
the Channel Islands with first hand
accounts by the people who
remember the years 1940 to 1945.

Roy McLoughlin

STARLIGHT PUBLISHING

First published in May 1995. Reprinted in July 1995,
August 1996, January 1998, April 1999,
and June 2000 by Starlight Publishing.

Unit 3B Barette Commercial Centre,
La Route du Mont Mado
St John, Jersey JE3 4DS.

Cover design and overall production by Simon Watkins
Page design and typesetting by Ex Libris Press,
Bradford on Avon, Wiltshire
Printed by Cromwell Press, Trowbridge, Wiltshire

ISBN 0 9525659 0 0

Publisher's Note

Efforts were made to obtain permission to quote two short excerpts from
Islands in Danger by Alan and Mary Seaton Wood amounting to five and
twenty-one words respectively. The copyright was orginally held by
Evans Brothers of 2A Portman Mansions, Chiltern Street, London, W1.
This firm advises that it does not possess records relating to the original
publication in 1955 of *Islands in Danger* and that, in place of its
authorization, this proviso should be published here.

To

Ada and Donald Le Gallais

whose many recollections inspired this book.

*For historical supervision
the publisher's thanks are due to*

Michael Ginns M.B.E.

of the Channel Islands Occupation Society.

...the tumult and the shouting dies;
the captains and the kings depart...

Kipling's Recessional

...the race is not to the swift
nor the battle to the strong...

Ecclestiastes IX

Time and the hour run through
the roughest day...

Macbeth. Act 1, Scene 3.

CONTENTS

List of Illustrations

Plates: Pages 2, 35-50, 78-86, 113-126, 165-170

We acknowledge with thanks permission to
reproduce photographs supplied by

Bundesarchiv, Germany
Carel Toms Collection
Channel Islands Military Museum
Imperial War Museum
Jersey Evening Post
Société Jersiaise Photographic Archive
Channel Islands Occupation Society
Priaulx Library, Guernsey
Richard Mayne Collection

PART 1

THE PEOPLE

with grateful acknowledgements to all persons interviewed.

CHAPTER 1

Opening Moves

THE YEAR 1940 is simply a date in the history books for most people of the generation born since the war. For them it stands for a list of historical events - the evacuation from Dunkirk, the Battle of Britain and the blitz on London. But for others living at the time 1940 marked the beginning of a new chapter in their lives. There are men and women in the Channel Islands whose memories will always go back to the Nazi Occupation in all its phases, from the invasion under the blue skies of midsummer to the dramatic last days five years later as Hitler's army collapsed in the ruins of Germany.

Islanders who were then children or teenagers will never forget the sight of German soldiers marching in the streets of St. Helier and St. Peter Port, accompanied by the blaring brass of military bands. A few Sarkees still speak of troops in uniform kit strolling along the Avenue or patrolling the Sark cliffs.

It all happened long ago and now seems as insubstantial as a dream. With the passing years more and more people disappear from the ranks of the living and their memories of the German Occupation go with them. Yet it seems that an account of the years 1940 to 1945 should contain the personal experiences of individuals in the Islands while relating them to the wider perspective of Europe at war. Victories and defeats as great armies pursue each other across the Continent and in Africa provide a matrix for the main events of the time but a closer view of what the conflict did to life in the Channel Islands shows what is now history in human terms. The realities of daily life under an alien military power, with all its rules and regulations, brings into focus both Islanders and Germans in this ill-assorted wartime community.

It was in the nineteen thirties that the first signs appeared of the storm to come when a tidal wave of conquest would sweep over western Europe and eventually engulf the Channel Islands. Hitler became Chancellor of Germany in 1933. Almost at once the new Nazi administration took over the Army and civil affairs, extending to total control of newspapers, books, radio and films, thus ensuring that Hitler's message went out loud and clear to everyone in the land.

As if this were not enough, the new Minister of Propaganda, Dr Joseph Goebbels, devised the spectacle of the mass rally where marching troops, speeches and patriotic songs aroused a wild adoration of the Führer among the thousands assembled on these occasions and spread a powerful nationalism throughout the country among millions listening to the radio.

Every Nazi rally had as its climax the appearance of Hitler himself, stage managed by Dr Goebbels to look like a miraculous visitation. When Hitler spoke he mesmerised his people as if gifted with a strange power even though his actual words were hardly more than an hysterical repetition of boasts, threats and accusations against the leaders of neighbouring countries. At the Berlin Sports Palace in 1937 he addressed the rally in his typical theatrical style.

> *Germany will take its rightful place in the world. I make this promise to the German people. I shall never submit my destiny and the destiny of Germany to the dictates of those in Europe who call themselves statesmen. These small-minded nonentities cannot even provide their own people with the necessities of life and yet they rule three quarters of the world. They are the men of 1918 who betrayed the German nation. I will not allow Germany to contribute to the profits of the London Stock Exchange and international Jewry. This infamous plutocratic clique would condemn us to starvation. But such crimes cannot go on. Our army will have the greatest, the most modern weapons in the world. I promise this. We shall be united in our struggle for a greater Germany. Ein Volk. Ein Reich. Ein Führer.*

The applause, the shouts and the fanfares which always followed a Hitler speech and the well-drilled chorus of *Sieg Heils* should have warned the

Governments of Britain and France that a dangerous beast was stirring the heart of Germany. But disagreements between politicians, both British and French, caused a paralysis among those trying to work out a policy for dealing with the Nazi menace.

In the meantime, the German Army was on the move. It had marched into the demilitarised zone of the Rhineland against the provisions of an international treaty. To Hitler international treaties were merely scraps of paper to be torn up when inconvenient. Austria was the next to be taken over - then the German speaking area of Czechoslovakia and finally the entire country from end to end.

The governments of France and Britain preferred to condone the German expansion into Central Europe rather than risk a war. By the summer of 1939 Hitler was demanding the port of Danzig and on September 1st German forces crossed the frontier of Poland.

At last action had to be taken because Poland's frontiers had been guaranteed jointly by Britain and France. On Sunday morning, September 3rd, people all over Britain switched on their radio sets to hear the Prime Minister, Neville Chamberlain, make his fateful announcement to the nation.

> *I am speaking to you from the cabinet room in Downing Street. This morning the British Ambassador in Berlin handed the German Government a final note stating that unless we heard from them by eleven o'clock that they were prepared at once to withdraw their troops from Poland a state of war would exist between us. I have to tell you now that no such undertaking has been received and that consequently this country is at war with Germany.*

While the Germans were annihilating the Polish army in a drive towards Warsaw, a British Expeditionary Force took up defensive positions in northern France and the French Army occupied its forts in the Maginot line between Luxembourg and Switzerland. The autumn and the winter came without incident. All was quiet on the western front. In the early months of 1940 no one in the Channel Islands imagined that the war could spread over great areas of France as far as Normandy and beyond.

Jersey and Guernsey seemed far away from the battle fronts and hoteliers and guest house proprietors made ready for the 1940 summer season. It was business as usual. The Jersey Tourism office advertised the Island as the best choice for wartime holidays that year. In Guernsey a similar air of optimism prevailed. One Guernseyman said: "We never thought the Germans would come here. We realised we might be bombed from time to time but an actual invasion was unthinkable."

The first intimation of anything amiss came in the month of May when news of the German breakthrough into Belgium sent shock waves through the Allied High Command. In just over a fortnight the Germans had encircled the Channel ports but could not prevent the historic rescue of most of the British Expeditionary Force from the beaches of Dunkirk.

It was the first week of June when contingents of the German Army crossed the Seine at Quillebeuf. The Bailiff of Jersey, Alexander Coutanche, heard the news from the Attorney General who had a radio set in his office nearby. Quillebeuf was not so far away. If the Germans had crossed the river they were closer than anyone had thought possible. Coutanche went at once to the Lieutenant Governor who telephoned to the Home Office in Whitehall to find out what was being done for the protection of the Islands.

In Guernsey also the authorities reacted to the news. A number of experienced people in the States and in official positions combined to constitute what was called the Controlling Committee, headed by Guernsey's *Procureur* (Attorney General) who, as the Bailiff's deputy, had taken over the direction of civil affairs. His name was Ambrose Sherwill, a man soon to be personally involved in the Island's calamities. The first question was - should the population be evacuated to England and, if so, could the evacuation be completed before the Germans arrived on the nearby coast of France?

Events were proceeding at an ever accelerating pace in Jersey. The Lieutenant Governor received a War Office message saying that thousands of men belonging to the southern group of the British Expeditionary Force were stranded in St. Malo and in danger of capture by the advancing German Army. The Admiralty wanted Jersey to mount a relief operation with all available ships, large and small, as had been done at Dunkirk. The Jersey Bailiff, Alexander Coutanche, telephoned the Commodore of St. Helier Yacht Club and then rang the Harbour Office which alerted the Company of Town Pilots. The organisation of a little armada had begun.

On June 17th the first boats set sail. By the next day there were seventeen yachts, seven cargo ships (normally carrying potatoes) and a Royal Navy torpedo boat with a capacity for seven men. Across at St. Malo the larger vessels dropped anchor outside the port in the roads, being unable to get through the locks. It was the task of the little ships to ferry the men across to the waiting transports which then made the voyage back to Jersey. A total of 21,474 came out from St. Malo. The last to leave were the engineers who had stayed to blow up the oil storage tanks.

In Jersey rumours were going around that a mass evacuation from the Island was being prepared. Alexander Coutanche now showed his qualities of leadership as Bailiff. He made speeches at street corners in the town, in the Royal Square and in the country parishes, saying that ships would be coming for those who wanted to leave but, as for himself, he and his wife were staying on. He added that as long as the Union Jack was flying on the mast at Fort Regent he could offer everyone a degree of safety. And if there came a day when the flag had to be lowered he promised that he would be at the Fort personally to haul it down.

At this time of greatest peril for the Channel Islands there was little help from London. Whitehall was in a state of confusion. Different departments were following different policies. The War Office thought that the Islands needed nothing more than demilitarisation to protect them from bombardment. The Home Office wanted the demilitarisation announcement to be made at once to save the Islands from a German onslaught with consequent loss of life. But the War Office delayed the announcement which, they thought, would be a signal for the Germans to walk in.

The Director of Sea Transport understood the Home Office to say that evacuation was unnecessary but someone on another telephone line in the same department told the Bailiffs of Jersey and Guernsey that shipping would be provided for everyone. This was not the story put out by the Ministry of Home Security which declared that only women and children were to go. Finally, the issue was further confused by the Ministry of Food saying that there would be no food shortages in the Islands.

People in Jersey noticed that the soldiers rescued from St. Malo did not dig in to defend the Island. Instead they were sent back to England. The Lieutenant Governor, a General in the British Army, also went away as did all Navy and Air Force personnel in accordance with the demilitarisation order which had still not been announced publicly. An uneasy feeling of near panic set in. Local banks were thronged with people trying to draw out their deposits. £300,000 worth of bank notes came in from London to keep reserves above demand, even though a withdrawal limit of £25 had been set to stem the flow.

When the evacuation ships arrived in St. Helier harbour they added to the atmosphere of catastrophe which overshadowed the daily affairs of the Island. Leslie Sinel, author of the diary of events entitled "The German Occupation Of Jersey," remembers the ticket queues and the crowds milling round the harbour piers.

> *They announced the evacuation on the 19th of June. People could go to the Town Hall and get tickets for the boats which they sent to take away the population. Some went and some didn't. One wasn't too sure, exactly what to do. I had bought my house. My mother-in-law was seventy. My son was just born. It was a terrible decision.*

In Guernsey the number of people going away was somewhat larger than in Jersey but the passengers on the whole were very much the same - wives, children and young men of military age who were going to England to join the forces. But uncertainty and indecision haunted everyone. Unofficial posters appeared on walls in St. Peter Port saying: "Why go mad? There's no place like home." A Guernsey businessman, Frank Stroobant, has a vivid memory of those days of turmoil.

> *Many like myself stayed because we didn't know what to do. We were in a state of confusion. We felt that if we got the women and children out we could follow later - because we didn't expect to be occupied. We expected to get the odd air*

raid, like Malta, but we didn't expect to be fully occupied. Now, of course, I can look back and imagine why it happened. To the Germans - and particularly to Hitler - it was a fantastic victory, a propaganda victory beyond his wildest dreams - occupying part of the British Empire without any great loss of life. I must say, in defence of the Germans, there was no real brutality in Guernsey by the occupying forces. I always had the feeling that they respected the English. In fact, I think there is a happier relationship between the Germans and the English than with many other people because we are closely related. But there was still a lot of privation and things got steadily worse. And so I think the evacuation was an excellent idea.

Alderney and Sark presented quite different problems during this fatal week. The 1400 inhabitants of Alderney, isolated by distance and lack of transport both from Guernsey and England, were yet only eight miles from France. It was the nearest Island to the rapidly approaching enemy and sounds of gunfire were soon to be heard in the distance. To make matters worse panic stricken French refugees arrived in fishing boats with their children and their pathetic bundles of belongings.

The President of the Alderney States, Judge French, was an ex-soldier and a man of courage and common sense. To abandon the Island and take everyone away seemed to be the best course of action but he called a public meeting and asked for votes on staying or leaving. Almost the entire population voted for going.

Cattle and domestic pets were an immediate problem. The Island's farmers left behind six hundred beasts, some turning their cattle loose to wander at will. People took domestic pets to the butcher to be slaughtered. Finally, some householders buried valuables in their gardens before embarking on the rescue ships for England. They went with almost nothing. Two suitcases per person was the rule. Stragglers who missed the last ship clambered aboard the Guernsey lifeboat which arrived some days later. Its crew found cows wandering in the main street of St. Anne, bellowing with pain because their udders were almost bursting with too much milk. They were shot to put them out of their agony. Alderney was now a desert land with only remnants of its human habitation.

The little Island of Sark faced the situation in a different way. Its 471 inhabitants decided to stay put under the leadership of the formidable Sybil Hathaway, *La Dame de Sercq*. As Seigneur of Sark she possessed feudal rights over the entire Island and believed that she could manage the Germans just as well as she managed her own people. Her attitude to the crisis was summed up in a few words. She said: "One does not leave one's land."

Not far away German tanks rumbled across Normandy while the Channel Islands lay becalmed in the golden haze of perfect summer weather. In Guernsey the tomatoes were ripening, farm girls were packing early potatoes in Jersey and the buttercups and red campions flowered in the hedgerows.

CHAPTER 2

Raiders From The Sky

DURING THE LAST TEN DAYS of June three entirely separate groups of people were busy making plans. First, there was the War Cabinet in London deciding, on the advice of the Chiefs of Staff, to withdraw all detachments of the armed forces from the Islands as they could not be defended successfully against a vastly superior German Army. When the time came - but not at once - demilitarisation would be declared officially.

The second group was at German Naval Headquarters, Northern France. Admiral Karlgeorg Schuster of the *Kriegsmarine* had the task of supervising the invasion of the Islands because operations across the sea naturally fell to the Navy. His deputy, Admiral Eugen Lindau, was collecting intelligence reports and aerial photographs purporting to show military installations in Jersey and Guernsey. An estimate had to be made of what degree of resistance an invasion force would meet.

Distant from both the War Cabinet and the *Kriegsmarine* headquarters, a third group also considered the possibility of an invasion. The men and women still going about their daily lives in the Channel Islands were the people who had an overriding concern about the future. Many thought they might still be able to get to England if the situation became critical. Few could foresee how events would overtake them.

On the 24th June a letter from King George VI reached the Bailiffs of Guernsey and Jersey. It was expected to coincide with the long awaited declaration of demilitarisation but, in fact, its contents had not been made public on the radio or in the newspapers. His Majesty wrote as follows:

> *For strategic reasons it has been found necessary to withdraw*
> *the Armed Forces from the Channel Islands. I deeply regret*
> *this necessity and I wish to assure my people in the Islands that,*

in taking this decision, my Government has not been unmindful of their position. It is in their interests that the step should be taken in present circumstances. The long association of the Islands with the Crown and the loyal service the people of the Islands have rendered to my ancestors and myself are guarantees that the link between us will remain unbroken and I know that my people in the Islands will look forward with the same confidence as I do to the day when the resolute fortitude with which we face our present difficulties will reap the reward of victory.

This notification did not reach the German High Command and Admiral Schuster, in charge of the Channel Islands operation, assumed that troops and guns were still in place. He and his deputy looked again at the aerial photographs and decided to lay on an air raid to test the defences.

Late in the afternoon of June 28th six Heinkel bombers flew over Jersey and Guernsey, attacking mainly the harbours at St. Helier and St. Peter Port. Rows of lorries containing tomatoes were lined up on the quay in Guernsey. The Germans mistook them for military wagons of one kind or another - probably for ammunition, they thought. The lorries were standing on the north arm of the harbour known as the White Rock. Frank Stroobant who, among other ventures, ran a café nearby saw the air attack at close range.

We were all in the café. The first time I realised it was an air raid was when all the windows came in. They were blitzed by machine gun bullets. Looking out, we could see a blaze on the White Rock where all the lorries were burning. In the café it was a general panic - everybody on the floor. But after the first burst I managed to get them down into the cellar. I don't think the air raid lasted more than ten minutes at the very most. But we naturally expected them to return and finish the job off - which they didn't do. The air raid warden came in to me and said: "Frank, this is a mess." And I looked out and saw that by this time the White Rock was a pall of smoke. And that is where the casualties happened because many of the lorry drivers had, for safety, dived under their vehicles and, of course, when they were machine gunned the petrol tanks exploded.

At the time of the air raid, Guernsey's *Procureur* and Head of the Controlling Committee, Ambrose Sherwill, was in his office overlooking the harbour. He was speaking on the telephone to his opposite number in Whitehall, Charles Markbreiter, who was inclined to think that the Channel Islands were in no immediate danger. Sherwill broke off the conversation and held the telephone out of the window so that Markbreiter could hear the stuttering rattle of machine guns.

Over in Jersey a line of lorries on the quayside also attracted the attention of the bomber pilots. Again the Germans suspected them of being military trucks for transporting ammunition whereas, in fact, they contained potato barrels. As the planes flew in they ripped through the potatoes with machine gun fire and dropped bombs around the harbour, setting fire to Norman's store and warehouse as they roared over at almost roof height.

One witness to the havoc and destruction was Dr Averell Darling, the Resident Medical Officer on duty at the Jersey General Hospital. The afternoon of the air raid is still in his memory.

I was in the male surgical ward dealing with a patient when I heard the noise of planes. I looked out of the window and saw three Heinkel bombers. As I watched I saw bombs beginning to fall. I left the patient and went through the hospital down to Casualty. And almost as I got there the first victim arrived. He had a great hole blown in the side of his chest and he died within a matter of moments. Fifty per cent of those who were admitted to the hospital and who died were killed by bombs. The other half died from machine gun bullets.

Yvette Coley, of the Jersey Farmers Co-Operative, is another one who remembers the afternoon when the German planes came over.

At the time I was working with my father at the potato

warehouse on the New North Quay. When the explosions came there were falling bits of masonry and bricks from Norman's building which came crashing through our glass roof. The girls who were packing potatoes screamed in panic and I took them over to Castle Street where most of them lived. They wanted to get back quickly because some had children at home. On my way back to the warehouse the planes came again, firing their machine guns. I ducked down behind some red boxes that used to stand at the Weighbridge.

Another account of the air raid comes from Ernest Watson, one time Connétable of St. Clement.

I was in Kensington Place when the bombs fell on Norman's. From where I was – about half a mile away – I could see the smoke of a fire and there was a lot of dust just after the bombs. I could hear machine guns. It seemed pretty serious. I went straight back home to see if my wife and children were all right. As I was Head A.R.P. Warden in St. Clement I then went on to our headquarters at the New Era cinema. None of the other wardens turned up. They'd all gone to see the fireworks.

That evening Winston Churchill's War Cabinet released the information that the Channel Islands had been demilitarised. It was a case of bolting the stable door after the horse had gone. Twenty-nine people died in the attack on Guernsey and nine in Jersey. In addition, numerous wounded were recovering in the hospitals. Thus the Channel Islands shed their first blood in the catastrophic events of the forties.

The spatter of bullets and the smoke and debris from shattered buildings meant only one thing to the Islanders - that the enemy was at the door. To the German air force it meant something else. It meant that there were no anti-aircraft guns in the area and that probably meant no defences at all. Even so, Admiral Schuster at German Naval Headquarters could not believe that the British Channel Islands were without military defences of any kind. Besides, there had been no announcement of demilitarisation. It had been mentioned as part of a BBC home news bulletin but the Germans were quite unaware of it. Admiral Schuster thought that the lack of response to the air bombardment was probably deliberate and a trap to lure his forces on to the beaches where they would be picked off as they landed.

It was this excess of caution which delayed the invasion for a further two days. The Admiral and his deputy were brooding over intelligence reports while the German Air Force flew more reconnaissance flights over the Islands. A young pilot, noticing that Guernsey airport seemed to be deserted, came down and landed on the runway. A quick look round the main building confirmed that the place was empty. That was proof enough that Guernsey was undefended.

He climbed into his plane and flew straight back to *Luftwaffe* headquarters at Cherbourg where his commander hastily organised an invasion force of ground troops and packed them into transport planes for the flight over to Guernsey. There was some difficulty in landing because cows were grazing at the end of the grass runway but the planes scared them away and the Air Force commander soon established his headquarters in St. Peter Port's Royal Hotel.

Thus the German Air Force had the honour of being the first to take over a small part of Britain. This annoyed Admiral Schuster who was still assessing intelligence reports and planning a naval assault. The next stage in his routine was the dropping of three copies of an ultimatum from the air over Jersey. Surrender had to be signalled by white sheets hanging out of windows and white crosses painted on the Royal Square and at the airport.

So many sheets fluttered in the breeze from windows in St. Helier that the reply to Admiral Schuster was quite clear. No one wanted another aerial bombardment. The next day the Bailiff, Alexander Coutanche, was summoned to the airport to meet the Germans and receive the surrender conditions. It was time for him to haul down the Union Jack at Fort Regent.

Guernsey's Bailiff, Victor Carey, being elderly and not in good health, had abdicated from day to day decision making and had vested his authority in the Controlling Committee. Thus Ambrose Sherwill, as head of the Committee, became the man to surrender the Island to the invaders. The German Commandant for Guernsey was Major Dr. Albrecht Lanz, a well educated man with an interest in the arts and philosophy. He and Sherwill took to each other from the start, a fortunate circumstance which helped in the running of Island affairs.

Sherwill had been an officer in the British Army during the First World War. He had been decorated for gallantry in action and had nine war wounds in his body. When he first met Major Lanz, he brought with him his medals and put them down on the table, saying that he had once been a soldier himself and added: "I bitterly regret that I am one no longer but there isn't a rifle in the island. Now I realise that I must obey orders."

The gesture appealed to Major Lanz. It was the first step in a necessary diplomatic relationship.

The leaders of the three main Islands dealt with the Germans in different ways. Ambrose Sherwill believed in maintaining friendly relations and only in matters of serious dispute would he refer to the Hague Convention which laid down the rights and obligations of both parties in a state of war. In Jersey Alexander Coutanche was more formal, very much the experienced lawyer dealing with a difficult judge. He was feeling his way and finding out just how much power he could have as a leader of the Island population.

It was quite different in Sark. Whereas Alexander Coutanche and Ambrose Sherwill had been summoned to receive the surrender terms at places of the enemy's choosing, Sybil Hathaway, the *Seigneur* of Sark, did not even consider going anywhere to meet the invaders. On the contrary, they had to come to her at her house, the *Seigneurie*. She received the Germans as if they were foreign visitors coming to pay their respects.

Later she recalled the day when the first two German officers arrived. She was sitting in her drawing room and could see her maid across the hall opening the front door. As the Germans came in they wiped their feet on the doormat. That, she thought, was a good sign. From this moment on she had the Germans eating out of her hand, more especially because she spoke their language fluently. There were to be embarrassing difficulties later on because of a Commando raid which upset all good arrangements in Sark but that was to happen two years into the future. Now it was still the summer of 1940.

Reaction in London to the invasion of the Channel Islands varied from the matter of fact view of the War Office (that the Islands were of no strategic importance) to the colourful speeches of outrage by Lord Portsea in the House of Lords who said: "Fancy a British Government, an English Government, saying the odds were too great! We have heard of Agincourt....!" Winston Churchill was on to the challenge like a bull terrier snapping at the legs of a burglar. He sent the following memorandum to General Ismay, his Chief of Staff.

> *If it be true that a few hundred German troops have landed on Jersey or Guernsey, plans should be studied to land secretly by night on the Islands and kill or capture the invaders. This is exactly one of the exploits for which the Commandos would be suited. There ought to be no difficulty in getting the necessary information from the inhabitants and from those evacuated. The only possible reinforcements which could reach the enemy during the fighting would be by aircraft carriers, and here would be a good opportunity for the Air Force fighting machines. Pray let me have a plan.*

Churchill's eagerness to attack the enemy wherever possible took no account of the consequences of sending spies and commandos into the Islands. Guernsey suffered most. Sark had two commando raids later on in the Occupation and one group went ashore on the north coast of Jersey at about the same time without accomplishing anything. A whole series of nocturnal landings in Guernsey by agents in search of military information proved in the end disasterous for a number of people but mainly for Ambrose Sherwill whose efforts at keeping the Island running smoothly depended on a good relationship with the Germans. This was to be seriously compromised by the spying escapades of the next few months.

CHAPTER 3

Churchill's Missionaries

RECRUITMENT FOR THE DANGEROUS TASK of collecting intelligence material in Guernsey was among young Guernseymen serving in the British Army. Second Lieutenant Hubert Nicolle was the first of the spies to land. At the time of his posting to the Hampshire Regiment he did not imagine that he would come back to Guernsey until the war was over. But one day his commanding officer passed on to him an order that he should present himself at the War Office for a special briefing.

Details of a somewhat melodramatic project were given to him when he arrived. Would he be willing to go ashore in occupied Guernsey, spend two days gathering certain information and then return to the beach where he would be picked up and transported back to England? The officer in charge warned him that, since he would have to be in civilian clothes, he was liable to be shot as a spy if caught by the Germans. Hubert Nicolle accepted the challenge.

A submarine brought him to within two miles of Guernsey's south coast. The last stage in the voyage was made in a collapsible canoe in company with the submarine's navigation officer who was to take the canoe back after Nicolle's landing. Almost on the beach the canoe capsized in the breakers. They had to drag it ashore and empty it before the submarine officer could start back. Nicolle was left on the beach soaking wet.

> *I had no alternative but to take off my clothes and wring them out. Then I put them back on again and jumped around to dry them off a bit. The beach where we had come in was called Le Jaonnet. From there I climbed up the cliff path and hid amongst some trees until daylight. When dawn broke I heard a movement in a field nearby. It was a man I knew and he had*

come to milk his cows. I told him what I was doing and learned
that the only serious difficulty was the curfew.

My job was to find out what sort of defences the Germans
had at the airport. So I went to see Mr Mansell at the Viards
farm who I knew had fields all around and asked him to look
out for what the Germans were doing there. I decided I would
go to my home where my mother and father were because I
knew from there I could make all the contacts I wanted. It
would have been fatal for me to move around looking for the
information because I was too well known. People knew that
I had gone away and volunteered for the British Army and here
I was back in Guernsey again. It would have been a bit
suspicious. So I got other people to do the work for me.

Hubert Nicolle's father was in one of the departments of the States and
could give him a run down on the latest regulations imposed by the occupiers
and how they affected Islanders as a whole. His uncle was the harbourmaster of St. Peter Port and would give details of all ships going in and out and
what supplies were coming in. Next door to the Nicolle's house there lived
a certain Mr Collins.

He was the manager of a store called Le Riche. The Germans
discovered that Le Riche's had enormous stocks of food and
they went to Mr Collins and said – you will supply our troops.
We want two hundred rations for Fort George. We want fifty
rations here and we want twenty rations somewhere else. And
so Mr Collins knew the German strength. A few hours before
I left home to go back to the submarine Mr Collins came in and
said - there are four hundred and sixty seven Germans in the
Island, eleven of which went to Sark this morning.

Next, I had to get away. The plan was that the navigator of
the submarine would row a dinghy to our rendezvous on the
beach at Le Jaonnet. We had terrific problems getting this
dinghy away because it was in amongst the rocks with waves
coming in. We had about three attempts. Every time we pushed

*off a wave would come in and fill the boat with water. Then we
had to drag it up the beach and empty it. Eventually we got
away and rowed to the submarine which was a couple of miles
out.*

At the time when Lieutenant Nicolle got out of the Island two other
British agents came in. They were both subalterns and Guernseymen -
Phillip Martell of the Hampshire Regiment and Desmond Mulholland of the
Duke of Cornwall's Light Infantry. Like Nicolle, they landed in civilian
clothes and ran the risk of being shot if they were caught. A Commando raid
was scheduled for two nights later and the Guernseymen were to act as
guides.

The plan was for two main parties to come ashore, the first to attack the
airport, destroy planes on the ground and blow up petrol stores. The second
party was to land further along the coast and attack a machine gun post and
German billets. A third group would deploy as required in support of the
other two and try to capture German prisoners for interrogation in England.

On the night of the raid two Royal Navy destroyers dropped anchor five
miles to the south of Guernsey. The moon was hidden by a mist and
visibility was down to almost nil. A hundred and forty men of Number 3
Commando and Number 11 Independent Company left the destroyers in air-
sea rescue launches. But things did not go according to plan. The weather
turned rough and the operation had to be postponed for forty-eight hours.
There was no way of letting Martell and Mulholland know what had
happened and so the two guides waited in vain at their respective rendezvous
points.

Finally the Commandos made an attempt to land even though a heavy sea
was battering against the rocky shore. Two launches had to go to back.
Another lost its way and ended up near Sark because of a faulty compass.
One launch managed to deliver a party further down the coast which did not
succeed in finding its targets. Phillip Martel remembers coming back to his
rendezvous point twice more on successive nights but without finding any
sign of the raiding parties. Neither he nor Desmond Mulholland were able
to carry out their allotted tasks and their efforts had been wasted. Moreover,
the voyage out from Plymouth had been long and uncomfortable, according
to Martell.

I'm not a good sailor and I'd never been in a submarine before. When we were on the surface it was very sick-making. Things were better when submerged but we were a long time under water – the best part of twenty-four hours. Finally we left the sub in a canvas dinghy. We could see in front of us just a black mist but after a while there was the dim outline of the Guernsey coast. After I got ashore I could not resist the temptation to visit my home and my sister and her husband. I approached the house from the back garden through a neighbour's property. It was in the Queen's Road right opposite Government House.

As I was walking up one of the paths to approach the garden wall a German sentry suddenly stepped out in front of me. I thought - heavens, this is it. He didn't say a word. Of course, I was in civilian clothes and they had evidently posted sentries all round Government House because it was occupied by the German Commandant. It was a bad moment but I just walked on, climbed over the wall and went into the house.

The reason why we came to the Island was to do a reconnaissance for the Commandos who would be arriving in two days time and also to show them the way. The night of the landing came and Desmond Mulholland and I took up positions on two of the beaches. I was sitting on a large rock and shining my torch out to sea. But they didn't come. At one point an aircraft flew overhead. I have since learned that it was an RAF plane which was supposed to drown the noise of the landings. The Germans fired at it and this seemed to come from somewhere quite close at the top of the cliff. It certainly put the wind up us.

We had been told that if the landing didn't take place we were to go to the beach at Le Jaonnet where we would be picked up. But there was no sign of anybody although we came back the next night and the one after that. We found an empty house in St. Martins which my father owned and after that we slept in a barn. Then we went on to St. Sampsons to the Calderol, another unoccupied house. But we knew that this couldn't go on.

They had their basic rations which consisted of flasks of brandy, Horlicks tablets, biscuits and chocolate but their supplies were soon used up. After a week of this vagabond existence, tired and hungry, they decided that it would be best to give themselves up to the Germans. But they remembered that in civilian clothes they would be classed as spies. At their last gasp, they arrived at the back door of Ambrose Sherwill's house. They knocked and were surpried to be let in by Sherwill himself. He listened to their story and then asked them if they were quite sure they wanted to give themselves up. Yes, they were. They couldn't be hidden for long without endangering the lives of their Guernsey friends and relations.

First of all, they had to be fitted out with British Army uniforms. Sherwill went to a man he knew who had been in the Guernsey Militia before the Occupation and learned that a stock of uniforms existed in the Town Arsenal. On arrival there, Sherwill and his friend found the uniforms in a chest and soon put aside two which looked as if they would fit. Then Sherwill noticed the Guernsey Militia buttons. The Arsenal caretaker's wife did a rapid sewing job, changing the buttons for standard army ones which fortunately they found on the premises.

Martell and Mulholland, now in the uniforms, were ready to go to the German authorities. But would they pass an interrogation, Sherwill wondered. It was a critical situation in which his relations with the Germans as the man responsible for the Island population might be compromised. He picked up the telephone and got through to a senior officer at German Army headquarters, saying that two British Army officers had surrendered to him.

The German at the other end of the line was suspicious. How had they come ashore? Where were they? In Sherwill's house? How long had they been there? A moment of silence followed and then the German almost cracked Sherwill's story wide open. "Do you mean to say", he said, "that they have been walking about in daylight without being noticed?"

Sherwill could not admit that they had come in the darkness of early morning because that would have meant accounting for the eight hours while the search for Militia uniforms was going on. A quick reply temporarily satisfied the officer. Sherwill said the two men had changed into civilian clothes on coming ashore and these were wrapped in parcels and ready for inspection. Martell and Mulholland escaped the firing squad and became candidates for a prisoner of war camp in France. They had only just given themselves up to the Germans when Sergeant Stanley Ferbrache, also of the Hampshire regiment and a Guernseyman, arrived at night to rescue them but it was too late.

Ambrose Sherwill survived the incident, his reputation with the Germans still miraculously intact but the continuous interest in the Island shown by Winston Churchill and his Director of the Combined Operations proved in the end to be disastrous, not only for Sherwill but also for others involved in helping or giving shelter to the agents. No sooner had the crisis surrounding Martell and Mulholland cleared than another clandestine operation caused more difficulties for Ambrose Sherwill.

Second Lieutenant Hubert Nicolle who had successfully landed and then escaped a month or two previously now arrived from Plymouth by motor torpedo boat with another Guernseyman from his regiment, James Symes. This time the information asked for concerned the conditions of the Islanders under enemy occupation. Had any of them been taken away to Germany? What communications were there with France? How was the Island faring as regards food, fuel and medical supplies? These were the questions which Hubert Nicolle had impressed on James Symes before they set out because, at first, the plan was that Symes should carry out the mission alone. Lieutenant Nicolle remembers the briefing:

> *I was called up to London again and they said that the people at the Home Office wanted to know the general position in the Island – what supplies the Germans were bringing in and things of that sort. They said to me – you find somebody who knows the Island, put him in and a few days later get him out with the information we require. There was a friend in my regiment – Symes. I knew Jim well. We'd been at Elizabeth College together and I wasn't prepared to send him in on his own. So I went with him.*

They came in to Guernsey at Petit Bot and climbed the 300 foot cliff path. It was a dark night but both of them knew their way around and had specific places to visit – mainly relatives and friends where answers to the Home

Office questions could be easily obtained. They had three days in which to make their inquiries. The motor torpedo boat would then return, pick them up from the same beach and take them back to Plymouth.

It did not go according to plan. Nicolle and Symes went to the beach on several consecutive nights but no boat came. Perhaps the change into autumn weather with high winds had made it impossible. Like the others before them they were marooned and, with the waxing of the moon, the nights were getting lighter, Nicolle realised that another month must pass before the dark skies would return.

Even then there was no sign of rescue and the two men had been hiding out with relatives and friends for six weeks, becoming more anxious as every day went by because they knew that those who were giving them refuge ran the risk of imprisonment and possible transportation to the continent. In the meantime, yet another agent arrived - Captain John Parker. Shortly after coming ashore he fell into a trench by an anti-aircraft gun, making rather a clatter and he was promptly arrested by the sergeant in charge.

The Germans were now suspicious of everyone and in the circumstances justified in believing that many Islanders were sheltering British soldiers, some of whom might be spies. The list was already quite long - Nicolle, Martell, Mulholland, Nicolle again, Symes and Parker. In addition there had been an abortive Commando raid in which one of the parties managed to wander about on the Jerbourg peninsular without doing anything effective for the British war effort. Churchill called these escapades "silly fiascos" and reprimanded the departments concerned for their lack of practical organisation. In Guernsey the people involved were angry, especially Ambrose Sherwill. The British Government had abandoned them and left them at the mercy of the Germans. Why make things more difficult?

An announcement in the local press proclaimed that an amnesty would be granted to all British soldiers who might still be in the Island from the time of the demilitarisation and for those who might have given shelter to them. This was the result of a discussion between Ambrose Sherwill and the German officer in charge of the situation who wanted to avoid further evidence cropping up of his inability to apprehend any British refugees who might still be in hiding. He was already suffering from acute embarrassment over the escape of eight Guernseymen in a fishing boat.

The two fugitives, Nicolle and Symes, were still inclined to stay hidden in the hope either of being rescued or finding a way to leave the Island. But a retired Major-General, a Guernsey resident, advised them to take advantage of the amnesty which, now that they had British Army uniforms, would give them the status in captivity of prisoners of war.

It was the zeal of a high German official at the *Feldkommandantur* headquarters near Paris which altered the application of the amnesty and sent a wave of panic through all people in Guernsey who had any connection with the agents. The official became obsessed with the idea that Nicolle and Symes, now in a Guernsey prison, had come to the Island to organise widespread resistance. As a result he sent an order to the local *Kommandant*, instructing him to round up all suspects.

How many more spies were in hiding who had not come forward under the amnesty? The high official at the *Feldkommandantur* headquarters felt sure that the Island was infested with spies and resistance fighters. As a warning and a reprisal all radio sets were confiscated and the word went out that, if there were no further surrenders, twenty leading citizens would be taken as hostages and shot.

The Germans would not believe that Nicolle and Symes were a couple of ordinary British army officers. They would not believe that Ambrose Sherwill knew nothing of the spy ring. They would not at first believe that others were not still in hiding somewhere but interrogations among all who were connected with the escapade, including Ambrose Sherwill, yielded no more names than those already known.

Nicolle and Symes were to be shot. Ambrose Sherwill was taken to the grim Cherche Midi prison in Paris where he languished in a cell ten feet by eight for months of solitary confinement. Only the intervention of the Commander-in-Chief of the Channel Islands saved Nicolle and Symes from execution. He insisted that the Army should honour its amnesty. Over three months went by before everyone was released except for the two young officers who went to a prisoner of war camp.

Sherwill came back to Guernsey to find that he was no longer the *Procureur* and President of the Controlling Committee. The Germans would not trust him ever again. In London Winston Churchill told the

Director of Combined Operations to abandon his commando intelligence activities in any of the Channel Islands - at least for the time being. Very little had been gained and in Guernsey much had been lost.

"The storms of central Europe seemed far away from the Channel Islands."

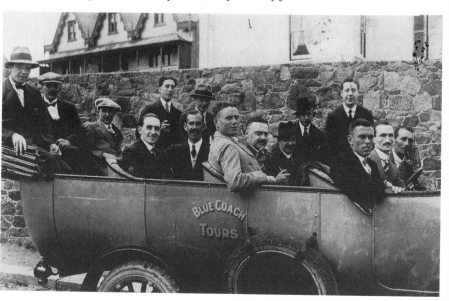

*28 June 1940 – Luftwaffe
air raid over St. Peter Port.*

Above: First Germans at Jersey Airport, July, 1940 (Alexander Coutanche second on left).
Below:A Messerschmitt 110 on Channel Island soil.

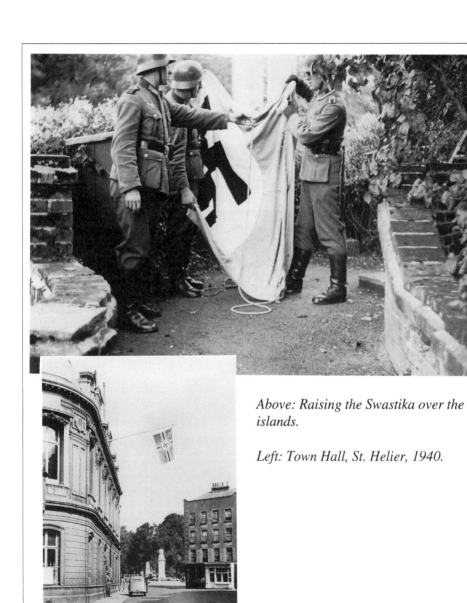

Above: Raising the Swastika over the islands.

Left: Town Hall, St. Helier, 1940.

Above: On guard at Government House.
Below: A show of strength – Charing Cross, St. Helier.

The sound of the jackboot in The Pollet, Guernsey.

Above: Look-out post near La Corbière, Jersey.
Below: No-go areas in the Islands.

MILITÄRISCHE ANLAGE!

BETRETEN, SOWIE VORNAHME VON VERÄNDERUNGEN STRENGSTENS VERBOTEN.

HAFENKOMMANDANT

MILITARY PROPERTY!

TRESPASSING AND ALTERATION OF ANY KIND WILL BE PROSECUTED UNDER MILITARY LAW.

HAFENKOMMANDANT

German pioneer platoon digging early type fortifications.

*Quiet time at
St. Ouen's Bay,
Jersey.*

Above: From Fort Regent – St. Helier Harbour and Elizabeth Castle
Below: Morning drill on the breakwater of Elizabeth Castle.

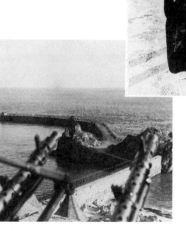

Above: Customs official of the VGAD (frontier control) at Gorey Harbour.

Right: VGAD official with Gorey harbourmaster

Defences at La Rocque Harbour.

Left: Colonel Graf Von Schmettow, German Commander-in-Chief, Channel Islands.

Below: Von Schmettow (now Lieutenant General) congratulating troops on successful raid.

Shops full of new treasures for the Germans.

Above: Let there be music.
Right: German military
band in the
Parade Gardens,
St. Helier.

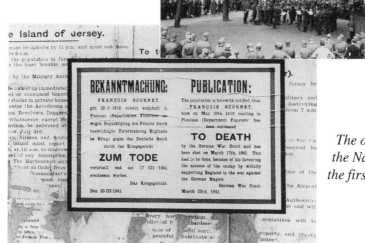

The other face of
the Nazi regime –
the first execution.

Left:
Sonderführer Holil –
censor at the
Jersey Evening Post.

Below: German
propaganda unit
with loudspeakers
– Charing Cross,
St. Helier.

German officers call at La Seigneurie, Sark.

Supplies come in heavily defended.

Parading in Marais Square, Alderney

Creux Harbour, Sark

CHAPTER 4

Ways and Means

DEVELOPMENTS IN JERSEY were on different lines. The Island escaped the attention of the Commandos until, over two years later, there was a single raid, as useless as all the previous Guernsey landings. The Bailiff, Alexander Coutanche, was above all a lawyer and he made up his mind that he would protect the interests of the population with every legal recourse to those rights which international conventions allowed to a conquered people in wartime. It was the only weapon to hand and it was to serve time and time again as the German occupiers increased their demands in the years ahead.

In July and August of 1940 there were no problems beyond the minor vexations caused by the influx of several hundred German soldiers - the disappearance from the shops of tobacco, cigarettes and luxury items which the invaders took over like locusts devouring fields of corn. There was a curfew and, later, bicycles and cars had to keep to the right hand side of the road but as yet the Germans showed no sign of falling on the ordinary people of Jersey like the barbaric hordes of Genghis Kahn. On the contrary, they seemed quite civilised and well behaved. Leslie Sinel, author of the *Occupation Diary*, remembers the impression they made on him:

We'd heard on the wireless how they'd come across Europe, terrifying people with the Gestapo and the atrocities in the concentration camps. We didn't imagine we would be treated any better. But, as a matter of fact, they behaved very well - at first, that is. Later on when the others came in with their secret police things got a bit harder.

Some people will tell you there was no Gestapo in the Island - only the Field Police. As far as I'm concerned, they were the

51

Gestapo. Some of my friends were interrogated at the Gestapo headquarters at Havre des Pas and I can tell you they really went through it. One man I know came out afterwards and he was white and shrivelled. You'd hardly have recognised him. So don't tell me there was no Gestapo.

However, that was later on. At first the troops behaved very well. In fact, the ordinary soldiers always behaved well. They were disciplined by their officers who told them not to cause trouble. Apart from that, they were cheerful. They were in a good mood. After all, they were winning the war. Think of the great success they'd had - sweeping all before them through Belgium and France. They were full of themselves. They believed that in the next month or so they'd be in England. But, of course, they didn't know Mr. Churchill.

The first months of the Occupation in Jersey went fairly smoothly. It was a time of adjustment to the new life which islanders were going to lead under the Nazi administration. Alexander Coutanche, in dealing with the Germans, found that a general air of good humour prevailed. Captain Gussek, the officer in charge of the invasion troops, settled administrative problems with a brisk nonchalance. When the Jersey Attorney General had to prosecute a man for some breach of a local regulation he asked Captain Gussek whether he could go to court and prosecute the prisoner as usual in the name of the King. Gussek replied airily: "Certainly – unless you prefer to prosecute him in the name of the German Reich. We have no quarrel with your King."

Two months went past and then the Military Government arrived, an organisation which always moved into any conquered territory after the Army had subdued all military resistance. It was known as the *Feldkommandantur*. The officials in its offices wore military uniforms but they were actually civil servants and at heart bureaucrats who soon began to increase the number of rules and regulations and issue endless forms and sheets of instructions. Captain Gussek said to Coutanche in his usual tone of irony: *Jetz geht der papierkrieg los.* (Now the paper war starts.)

It was the last time that he would speak to the Bailiff for he had orders to move on to other duties elsewhere. In his place came Colonel Graf von Schmettow, an Army man with a long professional experience dating back to the War of 1914. He was also an old fashioned nobleman from a land-owning family in Silesia. It was as Commander-in-Chief of all the islands that he took up his post in Jersey which thus became the overall headquarters for some time, later moving back again to Guernsey.

Colonel von Schmettow exhibited a certain hauteur in his manner. At the same time his behaviour was correct and typical of the class of men commissioned in days gone by as officers in the Kaiser's army of Imperial Germany. Alexander Coutanche was equally formal. Both men played a sort of diplomatic game, each in his own style.

One day Coutanche and his wife were out for a walk in the Noirmont woods near his house on the hill when they met Von Schmettow whose weekend residence, Cardington Lodge, was nearby. It was probably this encounter which convinced The Bailiff that he must make his position clear, as Sherwill had done in Guernsey in a different way. A little later he reminded the German Commander-in-Chief that they were enemies and could not meet socially but that this need not influence their behaviour when discussing official matters.

They met again in the German Army Headquarters, the Metropole Hotel in Roseville Street. On this occasion they agreed an arrangement which would avoid unnecessary disruptions of the normal day-to-day routine of life in Jersey. Coutanche drew the German Commander's attention to the likelihood of trouble because of the new laws and regulations which the Military Government had brought in. "There are bound to be misunder-standings," Coutanche told von Schmettow. "Let us now decide that when a problem arises we will not leave it to junior officials to make a muddle out of the thing. You and I will settle these disputes between us."

The German authorities had their own way of trying to make themselves welcome in Jersey and particularly in St. Helier. Military bands went marching around the streets and in the parks, making a cheerful, brassy sound, on and on, day after day until it seemed as if the Occupation had been devised solely to enable army musicians to practise their happy marching music. The Germans organised dances at the West Park Pavillion and else-where. On New Year's Day a special children's party with games and music was supposed to demonstrate their concern for family life. At the same time they executed a young Frenchman wanted by the Nazis in France. The boy faced a firing squad in the grounds of St. Ouen's Manor.

It was in the early period of the Occupation that people found leaflets fluttering on the ground in many parts of the Island. In Guernsey, too, leaflets turned up in lanes, on roofs and caught in the branches of trees. They had been dropped by the RAF and they contained the real news of the war to offset the biased versions printed in the local German controlled newspapers. The first batch contained a message from the King.

> *The Queen and I desire to convey to you our heartfelt sympathy*
> *in the trials which you are enduring. We earnestly pray for*
> *your speedy liberation, knowing that it will surely come.*

Teams of German soldiers went out scouring the countryside to pick up the leaflets before they could be found by the local inhabitants but this panic operation turned out to be quite useless. In any case, people did not believe the German news in the papers. Arthur Harrison, in charge of the Jersey Evening Post, remembers the system he introduced for casting doubt on any news story handed to him by the German censors.

> *The copy was full of little errors in the English composition.*
> *We always let these tell-tale mistakes go through to the printer*
> *so that people could easily see that the story came from the*
> *Germans.*

For people in Jersey, Guernsey and Sark the main source of news was the BBC which always gave the true facts in its radio broadcasts, even in items showing serious setbacks to the British war effort. Listening to the radio was still permitted at this stage of the Occupation because the Germans were not worried about the progress of the war. They confidently expected victory over the British although the much vaunted invasion of England had been delayed because of the losses in German aircraft during the Battle of Britain.

The *Feldkommandantur* issued instructions for the rationing of food. Two months after the arrival of the Germans an order came out for two meatless days a week and communal meals for children. Bakers had to use flour that was fifty per cent potato mash. Some people in Guernsey began to collect menus for a wartime cookery book based on the limited number of foodstuffs available. In Jersey people saved fuel by going to what were called community restaurants usually run by the States.

To supplement food stocks the authorities of Guernsey and Jersey created what was called the Purchasing Commission to facilitate the importation of food from France. Raymond Falla of Guernsey was the guiding spirit in this enterprise, working with George Vaudin and, from Jersey, Jean Jouault. They opened an office in Granville where essential arrangements were made for shipping their purchases to the Islands.

Raymond Falla travelled round Normandy and Brittany making deals with farmers and merchants. At the end of August he announced his first purchase - farm seeds for the coming season's sowing. He bought large quantities of wheat, barley, flour and chemicals for the waterworks. Soon afterwards he found another 1000 tons of flour, 15 tons of butter and 400 cases of tinned pork.

The States of Guernsey and Jersey soon realised that Raymond Falla was a rare type of commercial genius - part entrepreneur, part salesman and part diplomat. He knew how to swear in French and German, two talents he considered essential for dealing with delays at the port. By December there was enough food in the Islands for people to celebrate the festive season with the usual Christmas dinners.

While Jersey and Guernsey faced up to the problems of supply a different situation existed in Alderney. The Island was showing signs of life again. A lone farmer named Frank Oselton who had gone to Guernsey reluctantly at the time of the evacuation came back to his farm with a few cows. He found Alderney deserted except for a small number of Germans constructing gun emplacements for coastal defence. The Germans needed milk and were prepared to pay for it, thus giving Frank Oselton a ready market.

Another one-time resident, George Pope, came back with his wife, arriving in St. Anne in his converted lifeboat, having left at the time of the mass evacuation. Now that he was again on familiar ground, he reached an understanding with the Germans by showing them how to navigate between the island and a reef of rocks known as the Casquets where a platoon on guard at the lighthouse needed regular supplies ferried in. Pope then took up farming in Alderney where his wife gave birth to two children during the Occupation.

Growing food was at first the most important activity in this desolate isle. It brought back a living quality to the scrubby fields. Soon the authorities in Guernsey came to depend on Alderney produce to supplement army rations which were being consumed more and more quickly because of the increasing number of troops arriving in the islands. Alderney at this time presented two contrasting impressions. On the one hand, the simple agricultural work of George Pope and Frank Oselton gave a pastoral character to the landscape. On the other hand, the fortifications on the cliffs had all the drabness of military installations.

George Pope was so pleased with conditions in Alderney that he wrote a letter to the States of Guernsey, which to the embarrassment of the British was quoted on the German radio. He said: "We are and have been treated with the greatest respect and kindness by the forces occupying the Channel Islands." Frank Oselton made a similar statement and in Guernsey Ambrose Sherwill had said much the same on the radio at the beginning of the Occupation. It was only later that he got into trouble with the Germans.

To construct more fortifications and other military structures the German High Command in Berlin sent over the Todt Organisation, Hitler's construction department directed by Dr. Fritz Todt, the architect who had built the great German motorways in the thirties. At this time, 1941, working parties came to Alderney from Guernsey and Sark for various tasks - agricultural work and the repair and extension of the breakwater at St. Anne. This meant a coming and going with many pairs of eyes watching developments. The Todt Organisation constructed four camps for workers, one which later became a concentration camp for political prisoners from the continent. A woman whose job it was to deliver supplies to the camp spoke of guards beating their prisoners and of barbaric executions. But George Pope and Frank Oselton could not see what was happening behind the barbed wire fences, occupied as they were with raising crops and milking cows.

CHAPTER 5

The First Year

THE AUTHORITY OF THE GERMANS in the Channel Islands rested on a number of legal or military conventions which, as far as possible, conformed to tradition and laws. In the first place, the Germans claimed the right to rule by reason of their military victory in France. When their forces descended on the Channel Islands they ruled by right of conquest. Historically, this has usually been the basis of changes in international frontiers. In other words, if you have the force to defeat the enemy you can claim his territory.

But numerous other details had to be settled after this opening stage of the Occupation. Were the islands in fact a part of France? German legal specialists wanted to know what justification there was in presuming them to be British. To whom, precisely, did Channel Islanders owe their allegiance in strict law? Hitler insisted that, by the logic of history, they were citizens of France and that, as a consequence, his forces had liberated them from slavery under the colonial rule of the British. But there were other opinions.

According to an adjutant in the *Wehrmacht*, the islanders said they were neither French nor British but subjects of the Duke of Normandy, one of the titles of the British King. A German Lawyer who came to clarify the position wrote in his report that the inhabitants were English patriots though of Norman origin. He was puzzled by the medieval character of local laws with their references to feudal lord, feudal tenant and fief.

Confusion as to the historical basis for the islanders' constitutions was reflected in one of the new regulations imposed by the Germans. It decreed that, in church services, prayers for the Royal Family would be permitted but the National Anthem could not be sung without prior permission. It soon became clear that, in the German mind, the King and Queen and the Royal

Family were quite separate from Winston Churchill and the British Government. Whether the King was thought of as the Monarch of Britian or as the Duke of Normandy was, in the end, quite academic. Hitler acted as he thought fit. He ordered new laws as he wanted them. For all practical purposes the Nazi Government was supreme and all powerful in its conquered regions but to legalistic minds among Hitler's advisers the question of the consitutional position in the Channel Islands left one point unsettled. Were the islanders entitled to claim protection from the Hague Convention?

Hitler's advisers knew that the Hague Convention applied to a subject people whose government had signed a formal surrender. This the British Goverment had not done and only if the islands belonged to France whose Goverment had already surrendered could Channel Islanders qualify for the benefits of the Hague Convention. The dilemma was settled by a compromise. An instruction came from the office of the Military Governor in Paris in the form of a *Verordungsblätter* which decreed that if recourse to the Hague Convention was made by and for the Channel Island States the Convention would for the time being apply. And, of course, it would certainly apply as soon as Britain was defeated which the Germans thought would be quite soon.

It was in this atmosphere of uncertain legalities that Alexander Coutanche in Jersey and Ambrose Sherwill in Guernsey attempted to obtain a few concessions from the Germans. In Sark, Sybil Hathaway did not avail herself of any legal procedures. She had her own way of dealing with the enemy. Every German commander who arrived in her island was entertained with all the charm which La Dame was able to use so effectively and, before leaving, he was asked to sign the visitors book. The Germans agreed to everything she wanted.

Her visitors book soon filled up with names of high distinction such as that of the Prince von Oettigen. After signing, the visitors usually added polite expressions of appreciation of her hospitality – "Many thanks for a lovely afternoon" or "Always delighted with nice reception."

Years later when the war was over some people asked her if she felt embarrassed by these cordial entries in her visitors book. She answered such questions with typical self confidence and logic. No, she was not in the least embarrassed. There was nothing to be gained by opposing the Germans openly or being rude to them.

In fact, as it turned out, Sybil Hathaway was the only one among the leading people in authority in the Channel Islands who refused to counter-sign German orders if she disapproved of them, with the exception of one occasion when Jurat Lainé of Guernsey would not accept the Nazi anti-Jewish laws.

By the beginning of 1941 much had happened in the two main islands. A working arrangement with the Germans had been achieved in Jersey as a result of the diplomacy of Alexander Coutanche. The inhabitants on the whole learned to accept the soldiers in their midst. But in Guernsey the normal flow of events had been interrupted by the landings of Churchill's spies and commandos and Ambrose Sherwill was still in prison in Paris. People were getting used to signs bearing strange words in the German language. Few could understand the multiple words which contained two or three run together into one, such as *Oberkriegsverwaltungsrat* – a senior war administration officer.

The *Felkommandantur* put out a circular among schools asking how many children would volunteer to learn German. The response was quite good but it was difficult at first to find enough teachers and text books. Even for ordinary school subjects there were problems. Many school buildings had been taken over by the army and even those which remained could not be adequately heated in winter but the authorities in Jersey and Guernsey managed to keep children's education going despite the difficulties.

Learning German was not likely to meet any opposition in Sark where the school children were quite eager to have a new diversion to break the monotony of life on a small island. Sybil Hathaway informed the authorities that twenty-two of them were willing to take lessons in the classes which were soon to begin. As in Jersey and Guernsey text books were scarce and Mrs. Hathaway said it would be up to the Germans to provide some. As to the problem of winter heating in the schoolroom, she said that the twenty-two pupils could have their German classes in the *Seigneurie*.

One of the inconvenient developments in this first year of the Occupation was the confiscation of bicycles and privately owned weapons such as shotguns. It was natural for the German authorities to demand guns which might be used against them but the *Feldkommandantur*, with typical German thoroughness, collected weapons of every kind, including an antique blunderbus and a pike. The list of these weapons makes colourful reading. It covered the personal souvenirs of men who had retired to the Islands after a life of service overseas in various parts of the British Empire. There were spears, krises, assegais, kukris, cutlasses, hunting weapons of all kinds and museum items such as flintlock guns and halberds.

Possession of these cureos required a licence from the *Felkommandantur*, an organisation which proved itself reasonable in at least one case by allowing a retired colonel from the Royal Siamese Gendarmerie to keep a sporting gun given to him by the King of Siam. Every article bearing the slightest resemblance to a weapon came under the new regulations and had to be handed in. Those thought to be dangerous if they should fall into the hands of an assassin were held in safe custody and a receipt given to the owner. When the bureaucratic machinery of the *Feldkommandantur* started to revolve there was no stopping it.

The year 1941 also saw a worsening of the petrol shortage. All cars of more than 14 horsepower had to stay in their garages and then the *Feldkommandant*, announcing that petrol supplies were running out, banned cars of over 12 horsepower. It was the beginning of the end. Civilian cars disappeared from the roads. The Germans themselves were soon to need bicycles. A requisition order came out for a given number of bicycles to be handed in which brought loud protests from the island authorities.

In Guernsey the bicycle collection did not reach the required figure and the Germans accused those responsible, the Controlling Committee, of sabotage. Bicycles became a luxury, even those with rubber tubing round the wheels instead of tyres. The prices rocketed. In 1940 Damaille of Guernsey sold bicycles for £4. 19s. 6d. Within two years bicycles changed hands at £50.

Food was plentiful in the first weeks of the Occupation because thousands of people had gone away to England in the evacuation ships. In addition, the Guernsey States had arranged the import of goods and commodities to last for six months. Eileen Keen of St. Saviour's was then an assistant in the Guillle-Allès library of St. Peter Port. She remembers that the Town shops were full.

60

> *One could buy almost anything – not only food but dress material, shoes and things like that. People who had any money bought things with an eye on the future. So at first it wasn't as bad as it might have been. But then the Germans took over all the stock, mainly food, of course, and things got very tight.*

Stocks in Jersey were also relatively high immediately after the arrival of the Germans although not so evenly distributed throughout the different categories of foodstuffs as in Guernsey. For example four months supply of canned fruit was estimated and a year's supply of sugar. By this time the joint Jersey-Guernsey Purchasing Commission was bringing in supplementary items from France. Nevertheless the *Feldkommandantur* in its obsession with total control issued an order that all fowls over two years of age should be killed and used for food. The theory was that the sight of more poultry in the shops would give a better impression of the food situation.

Fewer potatoes in Guernsey caused some anxiety to the Controlling Committee in the spring. To make matters worse the *Feldkommandantur* ordered the dispatch of potatoes and tomatoes to France where stocks of these items were low. People in the country parishes began to grow their own potatoes and other vegetables. Town dwellers, having smaller gardens or no gardens at all, were not so well placed. But Eileen Keen remembers that, in St. Peter Port, people were generous in sharing what they had.

> *I benefitted from it – in that I was in the library all day and one of the caretakers gave me soup and little things they could spare. And my father would supply them with vegetables from the country. So we helped each other out.*

Soon the *Feldkommandantur* had set up its various departments - among them the secret police, the *Geheime Feldpolizei*. Members of this force (whom islanders called the Gestapo) busied themselves with preventing rebellion wherever they sensed that it might break out. One source of trouble, they thought, was literature. To stamp out heretical thoughts against Hitler and his regime they went to all the libraries and removed books which had anti-Nazi themes and all books written by Jews. This was a re-run of the tragic spectacle which had taken place in Berlin in the early thirties when the Nazis organised a public burning of thousands of German books. Rudolf Hess, Hitler's Deputy, had said. "When I hear the word culture I reach for my revolver."

But now in Jersey and Guernsey it was not only books which the Nazis feared. The *Geheime Feldpolizei* were on the watch for anyone speaking against the regime or expressing a hope for the ultimate victory of the British. They checked up on fishing boats and any other means of escaping from the islands. They even unearthed a light aeroplane in a garage in St. Peter Port. Although it was damaged and quite unairworthy the discovery led to an exchange of angry notes between the *Feldkommandant* and the Controlling Committee.

When a further search revealed two antique Russian hand guns in a store by St. Peter Port harbour and two swordsticks (used by Customs men when pricking bales for contraband) a new order came out signed by the Bailiff instructing all householders to search their lofts for weapons which might have been forgotten and adding a perfectly serious warning not to overlook any aeroplanes they might have on the premises.

The secret police were not part of the Army which was responsible only for defence and combat. They came under the *Feldkommandantur* and consequently were both feared and held in contempt by regular army officers. Nor were its men popular with civilians. In contrast to the *Feldpolizei*, ordinary soldiers seemed quite likeable. On the whole they behaved like normal human beings and had good manners. But Islanders had mixed feelings about treating them as friends and they were everywhere, in bars, cafés and shops. Some began to speak English and made friendly approaches. Then what was a local man to do – keep silent? Captain Roy Bullen, now the Jersey harbourmaster and then a child of five, experienced this mental conflict and explained it like this.

My father left the Island to join his regiment on the last mailboat to leave here. We didn't see my father, all of us in the family, until five years or so later. But there was a photograph always above my mother's bed of father in uniform. And there were German soldiers all around us. We soon became accustomed to them. Especially me. I was very young and could hardly remember anything else. From time to time if we were playing football - or playing any other game - maybe one or two German soldiers who were passing or working on some gunsite or other would try to join in and sometimes maybe we would allow them to.

But there was always this feeling of guilt – unease more than guilt because it's hard to feel guilty when you're that small – yes, it was unease about fraternising with them and playing with them. Always at the back of my mind was this uneasy feeling about these soldiers who, on the face of it, were quite friendly. But I thought - these are the evil people who were fighting my father.

At this time the number of troops coming into the Channel Islands was on the increase. In June 1941 Hitler issued a directive that the Islands should be reinforced against a likely attack by the British. In military terms this meant, at first, one infantry regiment for each of the main Islands, sixteen tanks and an unspecified amount of artillery. A month later Hitler discussed the Islands at a conference with his Naval chiefs. He said that when the war was over he would keep them for Germany. They would not become French possessions nor would he return them to the British. It was essential for Germany to have strategic bases in the Channel. The Islands were to be what he called fortresses - that is, fully fortified areas defended by all the most modern military hardware and, to all intents and purposes, impregnable - *Festung* Jersey and *Festung* Guernsey.

In October 1941 Hitler called another meeting with the chiefs of staff. He repeated his belief that the British would try to take the Islands for prestige reasons. Therefore the fortifications must proceed with all speed. Within a week of Hitler's staff meeting the entire 319 Infantry Division of the German Army moved into Jersey and Guernsey, followed by the military architects and construction engineers of the Todt Organisation. The Germans had come to stay.

CHAPTER 6

Secret Radios, Slaves and Deportations

THE CHANNEL ISLANDS were now locked into the Nazi system which extended over most of Western Europe from Norway to Greece. It was eighteen months since the Germans had first arrived and now, in the year 1942, the Islanders were to receive three severe shocks which showed that, however pleasant and friendly individual Germans might be, the masters of the Nazi regime had projects in mind which were to threaten the very lives of the people they had taken over.

Everyone felt, both civilians and local German commanders, that a change in the style of the Occupation had begun from the early months of 1942 onwards. The number of military personnel continued to increase and estimates put the figure for all the Islands at 25,000, rising to a proposed 36,000 on completion of the fortifications. For an official statement on the planned military strength for the final date there is no better authority than the *Armeeoberkommando* 15 whose records give the figures for the approved establishment. They show the Army as having 18,460 men, the *Luftwaffe* 9,500, the Navy 4,100, medical troops 3,800 and construction pioneers 11,400, making a total of 36,960.

In the meanwhile shiploads of materials were coming in and, in Jersey, Leslie Sinel notes in his Diary that, one day, he counted forty ships and barges unloading in St. Helier harbour. Week after week thousands of bags of cement arrived for ever-growing defence works – strong-points, bunkers, observation towers, gun emplacements and other military constructions, including underground store rooms and tunnels. In the summer of 1942 eight hundred tons of barbed wire came into Jersey alone. Guns of all shapes and sizes arrived – 101 light to heavy artillery pieces, 20 mobile howitzers and 9 medium, 165 anti-aircraft flak guns, 80 armour piercing shore defence canon and a variety of infantry support weapons, including morters, machine guns and rocket launchers.

In Guernsey a similar build-up of weaponry went on and, in addition, Guernsey had four of the largest guns in the Channel Islands, the *Mirus* battery, each with a calibre of twelve inches and a range of twenty-four miles.

Anti-tank traps, wire obstacles and mines spread along the lovely coasts of Jersey, from Belcroute, past the woods of Noirmont, to the little bay of Portelet, to the west along the great sandy vista of St. Ouen and northwards where gorse covered grasslands look down on primeval rocks, tapering away eastwards to the gentler seashore of Rozel. Over the verdant beauties of the landscape the hideous paraphanalia of war disfigured the headlands and beaches with gunsites and concrete walls.

The first of the shocks of 1942 was the *Feldkommandant's* announcement that all wireless sets were to be handed in at collection centres. From the beginning of July listening to the radio became illegal, the idea being to prevent people from getting news of the war. Some householders kept their sets and hid them in lofts, under drain covers and disguised as potted plants. Dr John Lewis, a general practioner in Jersey who, at the time of the mass evacuations to England, had stayed behind to look after his patients, found an almost foolproof hiding place.

> *I took some bricks out from the side of my chimney in the drawing room and concealed the wireless set in the wall. There was just the electric lead going in. That was visible but I managed to make it look like a connection to a hand lamp. I was certain it would pass if the house were searched. It was essential for me to have the news and hear what was going on in England and elsewhere. The Germans never found it.*

The penalty for illegal listening was prison and this might mean prison in France where anything might happen, including transportation to a concentration camp, never to return. But the need to hear the BBC news was stronger than any fear of discovery. To lose the radio was to be without the one lifeline to the world of sanity and freedom beyond the Channel. One of the hiding places was in a chapel in St. Helier, a vivid memory for Doreen Hills:

When the Germans wanted all the radios in we thought it would be a good idea, if we could, to keep one. So we managed to get an old one from an aunt of ours which we sent in under our name and my dad kept the other one. At first he wasn't too sure where to put it. Then, all of a sudden, he had a great idea – we'll put it under the organ in the chapel, he said. We were the caretakers of the old Wesley chapel. He put it here – under the floor boards. And he used to go up every night and listen to the nine o'clock news. Sometimes he'd go up through the vestry but at other times he'd climb in through the vestry window because he didn't want to be seen doing the same journey every night – they might have imagined there was something going on.

One day a German officer arrived. He'd been given permission to play the organ - every Thursday afternoon. Every week he used to come. We put the key in the vestry door so he could let himself in. Then he'd go upstairs and play - it was very good music - and when he'd finished he'd come down and let himself out. I never saw him but my mother did. There was a funeral one Thursday afternoon and she was just coming through the vestry after closing the church when she saw this German officer. He smiled and went out and although he came again many times, week after week, he never realised that he was sitting on top of a wireless set.

Some people who had given up their radios regretted obeying the order and paid visits to those houses which still had them. Ted Labalastier, ex-coxswain of the Jersey lifeboat, remembers the radio in his family home and the people who came to listen to it.

There were crowds of them who turned up at nine o'clock to hear the BBC news. They all came in. It was just like the pictures.

To replace the radio sets which had been handed in to the Germans a new kind of receiving apparatus appeared. It was not exactly new. People had used it in the early days of broadcasting in the nineteen twenties. This was the crystal set which could be made quite easily by following instructions put out on the air by the BBC. It required headphones because the sound level was low - and headphones were difficult to find. Instead people used earpieces from old-fashioned telephone instruments - thanks to the friendly help of men in the Telephone Department. In Jersey Donald Le Gallais, a baker of St. Ouen, made quite a number of these sets for trusted friends.

> *I had a dozen of these crystal sets at home at one time. I started making them because a man I knew had one which didn't work. I was on my bread round at the time and I went into his house because he told me he was having trouble with his wiring. Between us we got it going after we found a bit of copper cable. After that I went on making them and I sometimes got bits of crystal from coal. I gave a lot of these sets to my customers – at least, those customers I knew I could depend on.*
>
> *One day I got caught while I was testing a set for a farmer in his sitting room. A German walked in and I tried to hide behind the door but he pulled out his pistol and put it in my back. Then he saw what I was doing with the crystal set and he let me carry on. He said he wanted to hear the English news. Well, he wasn't the Nazi type and he knew the Germans couldn't win the war. He told the farmer that he wouldn't say anything about the wireless because he was going to come back from time to time to listen to the English news. In the end he was giving us sets of headphones.*

Father Rey of the Jersey Jesuits had a quantity of pieces of crystal which he gave to people. He even showed them to the German police when they came to question him. His manner was so charming and innocent that they went away, their suspicions allayed.

Leslie Sinel, author of the *Jersey Occupation Diary*, had one of these crystal sets. Before going to bed each night he placed the cat's whisker (a thin piece of wire) at the sensitive spot on the crystal so that he could get the

BBC news first thing in the morning when he would type out a summary for circulation. He often found that others had already heard it from neighbours. "The bush telegraph had nothing on us," said Sinel.

The same work of listening and typing was carried out in Guernsey but on a larger scale. A clandestine news sheet known as G.U.N.S. (Guernsey Underground News Service) appeared all over the Island and especially in St. Peter Port. Its circulation reached a hundred copies, one of which found its way secretly to the Bailiff's desk every morning. The news service was organised by Charles Machon, a linotype operator, and Frank Falla, an assistant editor, both working for the *Guernsey Star*. A roster for listening involved three others – Cyril Duquemin who worked by day in glasshouse cultivation and two carpenters, Legg and Gillingham.

A team of secret distributors circulated the G.U.N.S. newspaper. Charles Machon's mother gave out a dozen sheets daily to people she knew. The milkman carried one copy on his round for people to read before he put it back safely in an empty milk-can. Another copy lay between the pages of a book in the Priaulx Library in St. Peter Port. Those who knew the book title (which was changed every day) could easily find their way to the hiding place.

Three copies went to Sark, one to be kept in the back room of the Sark baker, Hubert Lanyon, for those of his customers who were discreet. Even some of the German soldiers in Sark could be trusted with the G.U.N.S. bulletin. They wanted to read the true facts of the war in place of the Nazi version composed by Goebbel's propoganda ministry. Hubert Lanyon once said that he trusted some of the Germans more than a few people he could think of. There was a thin dividing line between being indescreet and being an informer.

It was an informer, in the end, who gave away the G.U.N.S. publishing organisation to the secret police. The gallant little band was rounded up. Charles Machon received brutal treatment from the *Geheime Feldpolizei* because it seemed probable to the German interrogators that the G.U.N.S was not only a newspaper but a resistance movement planning rebellion.

Machon's mother took to her bed with an illness sparked off by the shock of her son's arrest. The Germans, with surprising compassion, let him out of prison to visit her, accompanied by an English speaking guard who stayed

68

in the bedroom while Machon talked to the old lady. They had only fifteen minutes for this last meeting, Machon told her. Hearing this the German guard said he would give them half an hour and, before taking Machon away, he told the old lady that her son was a hero.

Charles Machon died of ill health, starvation and brutal treatment in Potsdam prison in 1944. Joseph Gillingham died in prison in Frankfurt-on-Main. Frank Falla contracted tuberculosis and, with Ernest Legg and Cyril Duquemin, just survived the stomach agonies of starvation in a prison which was a staging post to execution.

For people in Jersey and Guernsey in the year 1942 the second shock was the arrival of foreign prisoners who were to work on the fortifications. The Todt Organisation needed labour in addition to the Germans and others normally employed. It collected a ragged mob of political captives, men and women from countries over-run by the Nazis, prisoners of war from the Russian front an international flotsam of refugees from all over Europe.

These bedraggled victims, wearing nothing but rags over their emaciated bodies and strips of cloth round their bleeding feet, seemed hardly human. They were ill, hungry and without hope. The Nazi guards beat them with truncheons when they fell over in the road from weakness, having come across Europe in cattle trucks and fed occassionally with watery soup and bread. One day a crowd of them were marching from St. Heiler harbour to a camp outside the town when they were seen by Joe Mière, then a teenager with a job in the Esplanade and now the retired curator of the German Underground Military Hospital.

In 1942 in the summer there was a commotion going on in the Esplanade outside. I went out to see what was happening, followed by some of the staff. There was a batch of forty or fifty slaves - Russians and Ukranians - herded along by the guards of the Todt Organisation who all held truncheons like pick-axe handles in their hands. Amongst this crowd was a woman and she accidentally dropped her precious bundle of belongings. She ran back to pick it up but one of the guards hit her across the head. She screamed and the blood flowed down her face, mixed with the grime. She screamed again as the guard hit her a second time. Then she had to run on to catch up with the column, leaving her bundle behind. Old Mrs Garner who worked for us looked up to the sky with tears in her eyes and said: "Oh, my God, where are you?"

During the next year the total number of foreign slave workers brought into Jersey and Guernsey was 12,000. Hundreds of these forgotten men and women slept in labour camps with little or no covering for warmth and hardly any water or food. Dr John Lewis of Jersey describes the conditions of the slaves in a camp at St. Ouen. After a day's work they lined up for water to clean the cement dust off their bodies which gave them eczema sores. Dr Lewis said that there was only one stand pipe and hundreds of prisoners waiting. Many of them did not get to their bunks for sleep until the early hours of the morning.

Jennie Seymour, a resident of Trinity in Jersey, then a child of seven, saw for the first time in her young life, some slave workers standing in front of the parish hall of St. Aubin.

There was a group of them, possibly about a dozen, shackled by their ankles, chained to each other. They were in a very sad state. Their clothes virtually hung on them - not exactly clothes but rags. I can remember standing there looking at them and then going home to ask my mother if the bread had come. We had one loaf each a week then. But my mother said it hadn't arrived. The first thought I had when I saw those people was to get my loaf and give them some bread.

The misery of working in the slave gangs led some of the younger men to break ranks and escape, hoping to find food for themselves. It was here that they needed help. Dr Noel McKinstry, the Jersey Medical Officer of Health, set up an organisation especially for the purpose of aiding slave workers who were on the run. He and Arthur Halliwell, the surgeon at the hospital, and Dr John Lewis formed a committee which compiled a list of "safe houses" – names of people who were prepared to take in the escaped men. McKinstry then provided the fugitives with identity cards by going to sympathetic officials at one or other of the parish halls and giving them a photograph of each man.

One of the names on the 'safe houses' list was Jack Le Breton, a farmer of St. Mary, to whom a number of escaped Russians had already come for food. His widow, Phyllis, remembers one they called Tom as a convenient nickname. He arrived one night, half starved and weak from exhaustion.

> *I was in the kitchen when he tapped on the window. We knew at once that he was another of those prisoners. My husband always gave them something to eat. I used to say to him - you're playing with fire. And my father-in-law was worried, too. He said - you'll get us all sent to Germany. I was very nervous but this particular one came to live with us. He was filthy dirty when he arrived but my husband gave him some clean clothes. In the evenings he would sit with me in the kitchen, learning English. He would say – what means this? What means that?*
>
> *At night he slept in our old car in the garage which we locked up permanently but there was a secret door. We trusted this man. He was the sort of man we could trust. The children loved him and when he could understand some English he used to read them fairy stories.*
>
> *Sometimes we would be here in the kitchen and we would see the Gestapo out of the window. Our Russian would go running out of the back door to hide. There were a lot of close shaves like that. The Gestapo often used to come. They didn't knock. They walked straight in. When our Russian felt that to stay with us any longer might attract attention he'd move on to another of the houses where he'd be safe.*

One of the escaped Russian slave workers in Jersey found shelter with the owner of a grocer's shop in St. Ouen, Louisa Gould. She took him in and fed him. After that he stayed some days in a room at the back. Louisa Gould had a curious feeling that fate intended her house as a refuge. The Russian was about the same age as her son who had been drowned at sea in a naval battle and she began to look on the strange visitor as a new son, heaven-sent

71

as a consolation for the boy she had lost. Details of the story are remembered by Harold Carter, a schoolmaster of St. Lawrence.

She decided to keep him for the rest of the Occupation. Of course, it was an indictable offence to hide an escaped prisoner. Unfortunately, she was given away to the Gestapo by an informer. That's what was suspected - someone who held some grievance or was jealous and wanted to get her into trouble from some feeling of spite. Louisa was taken off to the town prison and interrogated. The truth soon came out and Louisa was sent over to a German prison in France and finally to Ravensbruck concentration camp. The devils put her into a gas chamber and that was the end.

Her brother, Harold Le Druillenec, was a colleague of mine in another school. He also was arrested. At that time when one member of a family fell into the police net the rest of the family were investigated. They asked Harold whether he knew that his sister was hiding a Russian. And if he did why hadn't he reported it? The reply they got was that it was not an English custom to be a sneak, especially against one's own family.

He was taken across to France and then on to Fresnes prison in Paris. Eventually he arrived at a concentration camp near Friedrichshaven and finally ended up in Belsen – the death camp. It was full of dying victims, some of them dead already and their bodies rotting away in the open. The sickly stench was appalling, he told me. It was just when he was on his last legs at the end of the war that the Americans burst into the camp. He managed to crawl towards them on his hands and knees and call out: "I'm British." He survived, thanks to care in a military hospital and his own strong physique. Neither he nor his sister forsaw what would happen at that time in 1943.

It was natural for Communists to provide aid for escaping Russians with whom they felt a close political affiliation. The Jersey branch of the Party came into being because of the urgent need to help escaping comrades. Norman Le Brocq was one of the leaders of the movement and he remembers how the Russians were treated by the police, the *Feldpolizei* or, as they were called in French, the *Feldgendarmerie*.

The Feldgendarmerie were actively looking for any of these escapees and, when caught, they were beaten quite badly in the camps they were taken back to. In one particular example, a young fellow who, I was told, was only about sixteen was shot down in the the street trying to evade recapture.

A small group of us – speaking from memory, something like ten or a dozen young people headed by Les Huelin and to a certain extent by myself, formed a Communist Party at that time, really as a resistance organisation. One of its immediate tasks was to provide supplies of food and clothing for these escaped Russians.

One woman we knew, Mrs Metcalf who was Russian in origin, came here as a married lady in the nineteen thirties. She took it upon herself to teach a number of these young Soviet people - mostly Ukranians, incidentally, rather than Russians - enough English to get by if they were caught on the streets - purely colloquial English, nothing very grammatical but just enough to see them through a cursory examination.

She had one such young fellow, Mihail Krohim, in her flat – which was up a passageway and then up some stairs at the side of one of the town shops. Mihail was in the living room and she was teaching him some English when the Feldgendarmerie, possibly tipped off by somebody, were hammering at the outside door in the street down the passageway. Stella Perkins, her daughter, answered and they burst in. The noise and the clatter and the raised voices caused the upstairs class to end abruptly.

Mihail got himself into a cupboard at the top of the stairs and the Feldgendarmerie bunch burst into the living room and started searching there. Mihail slipped down the stairs and out into the street. There can't be a more lucky escape than that.

The third shock of the year 1942 came in the middle of September when a notice appeared in the local papers of Jersey and Guernsey. It said that all persons not born in any of the Channel Islands with their entire families were to pack suitcases and prepare to be transported to internment camps in Germany. The wording of the notice was quite unequivocal.

By order of the higher authorities the following British subjects will be evacuated and transferred to Germany.

(a) Persons who have their permanent residence not on the Channel Islands; for instance, those who have been caught here by the outbreak of war.

(b) All those not born on the Channel Islands between and 16 to 70 years of age who belong to the English people, together with their families.

To show that the order was official the notice bore the rank and name of the *Feldkommandant*, Oberst Knackfuss. The crisis had its origin in events which had taken place a year previously. In 1941 the British Government had complained to the Government of Iran (which was neutral) about the activities of German specialists in Tehran – engineers and professional people of that sort who had been assisting the Nazis in various ways. The British ambassador requested that the Germans should be interned or handed over to the Allies.

Hitler flew into one of his histrionic rages and threatened that for every German arrested one UK. born person in the Channel Islands would be taken to Germany and interned. A little later Hitler was again in a fury over the presumptions of the British and now ordered ten Englishmen and their families to be interned for every German. Estimates showed that there were 500 Germans in Iran at the time and if all these were taken into custody Hitler would require 5000 hostages from the Channel Islands, presuming the ratio to be 10 to 1.

The deportation order was delayed for a time in the pending trays of the Foreign Ministry in Berlin. Heads of departments were worried that if the order were put into effect German assets in the City of London which, up to then, had remained intact might be confiscated. Almost a year went by and then Hitler noticed that nothing had been done about the Channel Islands hostages. He insisted on immediate action.

It was not possible, even for the *Führer*, to speed up the processes involved which had run into a number of obstacles. The Foreign Ministry reluctantly made the first move but found that the Department for Sea Transport had no ships to spare as all vessels were needed for more urgent war movements. The Army was also opposed to the plan. Where would all these deportees be housed? There were no empty prisoner of war camps. In any case, military commanders objected to being responsible for women and children and especially for women who might be pregnant.

Hitler was adamant. His order must stand. After the difficulties had been overcome the order at last reached Colonel Knackfuss, sitting at his desk in Jersey. The *Feldkommandant* was startled, then alarmed when he realised what it would mean in his Island jurisdiction. But there was no possibility of ignoring the order. It had come direct from the *Führer*.

The chief of the defence forces in the Islands, Colonel Graf von Schmettow and other senior commanders of the local garrisons were deeply shocked and embarrassed. Hitler's order revoked the promise which the Army had given at the time of the invasion that respect would be shown to the lives, property and liberty of the Islanders if they surrendered peacefully and conducted themselves in an orderly fashion. This was a solemn undertaking which, if broken, reflected on the honour of the *Wehrmacht*. But there was nothing to be done. All the objections had already been argued.

The remaining question was the actual number of persons to be deported. Revisions to the original estimates had brought the figure down. In the end 1200 went from Jersey, 825 from Guernsey and 9 from Sark, making a total of 2,034. It was a sad and yet heroic time. The families embarking for an unknown future did so with commendable courage and dignity. Husbands, wives, children, old bachelors and widowers – all came into the deportation net. The departure scenes of the exiles are still remembered by Michael Ginns, then a teenager, now Secretary of the Channel Islands Occupation Society. When the news broke he was walking down Bath Street in St. Helier with his mother.

> *We met a friend of my mother's going in the opposite direction and looking as if a wall had fallen on her. My mother said: "What on earth has happened?" The friend replied: "It's a most terrible thing. We're all going to be taken away to Germany." Sure enough, outside the Evening Post office there was a copy of that day's issue in the window and an announcement said that all male inhabitants who were not born in the Channel Islands, together with their families, would be evacuated to Germany. It came out of the blue with no warning whatsoever.*
>
> *A German soldier was going round serving deportation notices on those people unfortunate enough to be chosen. There was no time at all to get ready for those in the first batch. Notices were served that evening. Some people were even pulled out of bed at midnight to receive their orders - and they had to be down at the Weighbridge for two o'clock that afternoon. It gave them no time to dispose of valuables, see that the house was in order, have pets taken to the Animal Shelter to be put to sleep, if they had pets.*
>
> *We were fortunate. We didn't go until the second batch so we had a little more time. Even so it was still a rush. The dog and the cat had to go to the Animal Shelter, the house had to be seen to and one had this terrible sense of urgency to get everything packed. In the middle of all this my father who was elderly and not in good health fainted. But this didn't do us any good because the German Army doctor in attendance at the Weighbridge said - "bring him round and get him in the boat".*
>
> *During the period that we were waiting I'll always remember a young German soldier – a studious looking fellow with his horn-rimmed spectacles - speaking a little English. He*

came up to me and said: "We're very sorry for what is happening to you. On behalf of my comrades and myself, I would like to apologise. It is wrong for war to be made on women and children."

Crowds gathered near the St Helier harbour for a last glimpse of their friends going aboard the ships. Suddenly people started singing the songs of those days, "We'll Meet Again", "The White Cliffs of Dover" and "There'll Always Be An England." It was taken up by those on the ships. The sound came floating across the water and then the fluttering handkerchiefs waving in the distance disappeared from view. The exiles had gone.

*Left: German
propaganda films
in Island cinemas.*

*Below: Books with
propaganda target –*
The Decline and Fall
of the British Empire.

78

Above: English-German dictionaries for easier communication.
Below: Build-up of troops in the Islands.

Above: Transport, 1941.
Below: Semaphore drill for the German Navy.

Above: Range-finder – Noirmont Point, Jersey.
Below: Anti-Aircraft practice.

Anti-Aircraft battery – Mont Rossignol, Jersey.

Above: Visit of Field Marshall von Witzleben (5th from right).
Below: Looking for fortification sites, La Corbière, Jersey.

Top: Equipment for the fortress Islands.

Centre and right: Work on making the Islands impregnable.

84

*Preparing defence points
for anti-tank traps, mines
and barbed wire.*

WIRELESS RECEIVING SETS

The public are reminded that all declaration forms concerning Wireless Receiving Sets must be delivered to the office of the Department of Essential Services, 10/12 Beresford St., not later than noon to-morrow (Sat.) November 16th.

W. S. LE MASURIER,
President,
Department of Essential Services

Above: The day the BBC was 'verboten'.
Below: Old type radio set in German collection.

CHAPTER 7

The Year of Fate

IT WAS IN THE THIRD YEAR of the Occupation - the last part of 1942 and on into 1943 – when people heard that the Germans were losing on all the battle fronts of the war. Hidden radios carried the news of Russian, British and American successes in halting the once irresistible drive of the Nazi war machine.

On October 23rd General Montgomery launched his offensive at El Alamein, surging westward against Rommel's Afrika Korps through Sidi Barrani, Tobruk and Tripoli. On November 7th the Americans landed at Algiers, Oran and Casablanca where many of the Algerian French joined them. The French navy in Toulon scuttled the fleet to prevent its falling into the hands of the Germans. In February General von Paulus surrendered the German Sixth Army to the Russians at Stalingrad and elsewhere in the vast territories of the Soviet Union the German drive to the East was bogged down in snow and mud.

In Jersey the Feldkommandant's ban on radio listening by the Islanders now included German soldiers as well, not only because of the news from North Africa and Russia but also because of massive air raids on the German homeland. The RAF's thousand bomber raid on Cologne was followed by a continuous saturation bombing of war manufacturing centres. Destruction rained down on the great German cities of the west – Essen, Bremen, Stuttgart, Emden and Osnabruck. The nightly pounding by the RAF, joined by day by the United Sates Air Force, reduced buildings to rubble with broken roofs open to the sky. 900 tons of bombs came down on Krupp's factories in the Ruhr, devastating 160 acres of industrial property. There were soldiers in the Channel Islands who had their wives and families in the stricken areas.

The Progress of the Allies made little immediate difference to life in the

Islands except that people could now imagine a future when the Occupation would come to an end. It was, in fact, the news coming through illegal crystal sets and other receivers which kept up the islanders' spirits and, since the information spread to the Germans, it also undermined morale in the occupying forces. In some places, particularly in Sark, German soldiers came quite openly to ask what the latest news was.

Rationing had, of course, been a feature of day-to-day life from the beginning but now the food shortages had the effect of increasing the number of burglaries. In 1942 sixty thefts a week were reported to the police in Guernsey, mainly food. Farmers had to guard their cows to prevent troops or escaped slave workers from helping themselves to milk at the source. Thieves stole chickens, goats, rabbits, pigs and general foodstuffs such as grain, even soap. The worst aspect of the thieving was fear. It was dangerous for a farmer or householder to defend his goods and belongings. He might be shot at or receive a blow from a hard object in the hands of an escaped foreign worker.

In 1943 the shortage of food induced many people to experiment with recipes based on seaweed and other unusual ingredients. Louise Board of St. Saviour's in Guernsey remembers her carrageen moss pudding.

We used to make a blancmange out of carrageen moss. This moss which is a kind of seaweed had to be dried and then crumbled up into a powder. You put this into a saucepan with milk and it makes something like a blancmange. Very nourishing - it has a wide range of nutrients but I started taking it because I had lost the lining of my stomach and this carrageen moss with milk restored it for me.

The moss would come ready ground from the chemist. That was the only way you could get it then because it was impossible to go down on any of the beaches. They were mined.

Sometimes we could get sugar beet. If you boiled it over and over again it turned into treacle. That was another way of sweetening things when there was no sugar.

We used to grate carrots and mix them with grated potatoes and oats. This made a quite tasty steam pudding. And you could also have carrot tea.

Food was one of the commodities exchanged in a system of barter which started when retailers could no longer replenish their bare shelves. Apart from food, supplies were running out of articles such as tea pots, towels and wearing apparel.

Announcements of second-hand goods for barter appeared in the local press. Sometimes shopkeepers played the part of agents in this emergency commerce. They looked after various articles whose owners had left notes saying what they would like in exchange. An electric toaster might be offered for a pair of silk stockings and the shopkeeper would receive a commission in deutschmarks. For a time it was a thriving business but after two years the Germans ordered a limit to the articles on offer.

The daily twists and turns of making do with what you could get is still remembered by Rosemary Martell of Torteval in Guernsey.

There was a great barter going on through the newspaper. Some people would say they had stored up some sugar and they would want a coat or a pair of shoes. But apart from food shortages, we ran out of coal. Then we had to find something else. We went wooding. In the autumn there were branches of trees blown down by the gales. We collected those. To economise on what fuel we had we did part of the cooking in hayboxes. You boiled up your saucepan – soup or something – and when it was ready you put it in the haybox and the hay warmed it. We also had a sawdust box – a big biscuit tin from the grocer's – and that had the same effect of keeping the heat in.

In Jersey Donald Le Gallais of St .Ouen had another method of emergency cooking. It was a sort of barbecue in the garden outside the house.

When we could get it we used wood for fuel as there was hardly any coal at that time. I had an old tar drum cut in half. I put iron bars along the top to make a grill. It could also heat an oven which I made out of a tin box. We couldn't light it in the house because of all the smoke and smell.

> *One evening we were cooking a special Occupation dish con-*
> *sisting of tomatoes and potatoes. They were just frying nicely*
> *and almost ready when, all of a sudden, a German officer came*
> *round the corner of the house. He wanted to know what we*
> *were doing outside as it was after curfew time, although he*
> *could see we were cooking our evening meal. But the curfew*
> *was more important for him so he kicked the whole lot over and*
> *we had to go without our supper. Some of them were like that.*

One day Donald Le Gallais was with a farmer and they came upon some railway sleepers in a field:

> *The Germans had brought a load of these sleepers up near our*
> *place. They were going to run a train from Ronez to Les*
> *Landes. So being that we were short of wood we thought that*
> *we would help ourselves to a few. They had a lovely strong*
> *smell like pine, I remember. A couple of days later the Germans*
> *turned up, asking everyone about the sleepers. The farmer said*
> *he knew nothing about them but the Germans searched in his*
> *shed and found a pile. They took no excuses and he ended up*
> *in prison for a month.*
>
> *The following week a friend of ours came out from town to*
> *see us. On her way she saw a pile of these sleepers in a gate-*
> *way. So, even though they were heavy, she managed to drag*
> *them to our house. She said – I found these and now we can heat*
> *up those baked beans. You should have seen her face when we*
> *told her that the farmer across the road had just been sent to*
> *prison for a month.*

The search for wood to burn became a regular daily task among women, something like going shopping, as Marcella Darling of Jersey recalls:

> *Nobody can understand who wasn't here at the time how very*
> *important a piece of wood was. Nowadays we look at wood as*
> *wood. But in those days we needed it as fuel. Occasionally the*

*men would get a permit to fell a tree and they'd bring home
some green wood which wouldn't burn very well. If we picked
up a piece of old wood it was a help for the fire - and we had
an open fire in our home. A fire like that would boil a kettle full
of water. In that we took a bath - a stand up strip bath with a
kettle of water, if we were lucky. Not everybody had wood for
boiling a kettle just for that luxury and on those occasions we
had to use cold water. Day after day you felt you would love
to have a real bath instead of washing in a kettle of water.*

Marcella Darling also thinks of shoes and how difficult it was to replace
them:

*When shoes wore out people had them resoled with things like
motor tyres – anything that would do. But smart fashionable
shoes were really valuable. I can remember exchanging a pair
of shoes that I was rather fond of. Some other woman had her
eyes on them. She said: "I will give you..." I forgot what... it
might have been a piece of black market pork, something in the
edible line... I liked those shoes and, foolishly, I parted with
them.*

A woman had to keep up her morale as best she could in the dreary days
of the Occupation and faced the problem of inventing new clothes, as
Marcella Darling remembers.

*We used old dresses. We turned them inside out, cut them out
again and made them up as new. I can remember one dress that
I wore. It had been a bright green which I didn't really like. I
dyed the skirt part of it a sort of petrol blue and used the top part
for a new jacket. The whole thing was inside out – pre war
material of good quality.*

*I had a friend who did a lot of knitting and she used to undo
old woollen garments and knit them up in completely new
styles.*

91

One person who had no problems with her clothes was a Jersey woman known to some as Ginger Lou, the girl-friend of a high-ranking German officer. While other women had to be content with altering dresses they had worn for years, Ginger Lou took over anything she fancied from the wardrobes of the wealthy who had left the Island just before the Germans arrived and her shoes came from the Faubourg St. Honoré. The gallant Dr John Lewis who had stayed in the Island in 1940 with his patients often saw Ginger Lou flaunting her finery in the streets of St. Helier.

She had identified herself completely with the master-race and went about in a chauffeur driven car because she was the mistress of one of the high-ups. She used to appear in the town looking like a fashion plate. If she saw a queue of people trying to buy, perhaps, one egg or whatever it was, she would just go to the head of the queue and say that she would have all the eggs that were there. And of course, she had the backing of her lover. After that the queue would have to disperse.

Shortages not only of food items but also of drugs at the Jersey Hospital were beginning to have serious consequences. A supply of insulin had been ordered from Germany but on its way through France it had been stolen by agents of the black market and diabetic patients died for the lack of it.

For surgical operations the Electricity Company fed a special supply to the hospital at the cost of blacking out other parts of the Island. It was at this time, according to the then Resident Medical Officer, Dr. Averell Darling, that the nurses used to do their rounds at night sharing a hurricane lamp.

The constant trickery in the quest for food became a life-style. When people met in each other's houses they would compare notes on which of the black market merchants had a stock of a certain item. Deceiving the Germans in order to get food officially allocated to the garrisons was a deadly game being played all the time. In Guernsey, Raymond Falla, in charge of agricultural arrangements, kept two sets of books – one for the Guernsey States and the other for the Germans.

Farmers had ways of keeping back a pig or two for themselves instead of showing them on the official register.

But they had to be on the watch for visiting inspectors from the Department of Agriculture or the *Feldkommandantur*. Peter Frampton, now an amusement arcade manager, was a teenager during the Occupation. He was working with his father, a butcher, partly in the shop and partly on special black market deals. They were nearly caught at a Jersey farm when they were about to carve up two slaughtered pigs.

> *We had these pigs on the kitchen table and we were just preparing to cut them up, my father and I, when all of a sudden we looked out of the window and saw German soldiers – a patrol of some kind. They obviously were coming to search the place. So, immediately we thought – what the heck are we going to do? Then – quick thinking – we got the farmer's wife, the dear lady, and said – upstairs quick and go to bed. Then we hunked the pigs over our shoulders, threw them into the bed with her and covered them over. There was a loud banging on the door and the Germans came in. We said – please do not make any noise because the lady upstairs is going to have a baby. So the officer in charge went up and the lady in the bed started moaning and groaning. The officer said – it's all right, we will leave you. Thank you very much. Sorry to have caused you any trouble.*

Illegal radio listening continued and brought news of the Allied armies in Italy although individual listening in Guernsey could not fill the gap left by the disappearance of the G.U.N.S. news sheets which had, of course, ceased publication with the arrest of Charles Machon, Frank Falla and their fellow resistance workers.

Jersey, too, had its heroes of the hidden radio. Canon Cohu, a man of immense courage and goodwill, kept a radio set in his church, St. Saviour's. He was a retired chaplain from the Indian Army with an unshakeable faith in Britain and the British Empire. He would retail the BBC news to people he passed in the street and, when visiting any of his parishioners in hospital, would take his notes of the news on a piece of paper slipped into the pages of his Bible. The Germans sent him to prison on the continent and he never came back.

Peter Painter, a business man, had a radio and was arrested with his son when it was discovered. Edward Ross, a dentist, and his wife, Nan, fell into the hands of the secret police because, in the first place, they were giving food to starving Russian slave workers. Then a search of their house revealed a radio. Like Canon Cohu and Peter Painter, they were drawn into the continental network of prisons and concentration camps.

The winter of 1943, going into the early months of 1944, seemed long and dark. When candles disappeared from the shops some people used diesel oil in old tobacco tins with a hole in the top and a shoe lace threaded through to serve as a wick. The gas supply in Jersey was available for only a few hours a day and people continued scavenging for wood or they used sawdust soaked in tar, according to Doreen Hills of St. Helier.

My Mother used to go to the gasworks. She would get a bucket of tar for sixpence and bring it back home to pour over the wood or sawdust or whatever we had. Of course, that made a terrible mess of the grate.

Food prices, even on the official market, were steadily rising. Meat in Jersey was 11 shillings a pound in 1942 and a year later it had risen to 15 shillings. Sugar went up from 12 shillings and sixpence a pound to 16 shillings and then on to 20 shillings. Butter was 25 shillings a pound in 1942 and 30 shillings in 1943, rising to 50 shillings by the end of the Occupation.

Black market prices were even higher. It was a risky business for those engaged in it. There were fifty black market prosecutions in Guernsey in 1943 and over a hundred in 1944. Anyone discovered keeping a pig without having registered it with the Farm Produce Board had to pay a fine of £5 or spend five weeks in prison. An illegally slaughtered pig attracted a fine of £10 or ten weeks in prison.

The Germans cut off the water supply at 5 pm. in St. Helier and this had disastrous consequences in the middle of January. De Gruchy's Store in King Street was in flames. The fire brigades of St. Helier, St. Aubin and Gorey arrived on the scene but half an hour went by before water came through the hosepipes.

Everyone felt a mounting tension as winter gave way to spring. The

Feldkommandant added new restrictions to daily living. More people were arrested for radio listening and the authorities organised a police trap for black marketeers. It was as if Hitler's officials lived in a state of continual nervous anxiety. Their Army and Navy Intelligence intercepted messages suggesting that the Allies would soon launch a massive invasion of the French coast and Hitler's best generals, von Rundstedt and Rommel, prepared to defend the western boundaries of the Reich.

CHAPTER 8

Islands Under Siege

ALLIED DECEPTION TACTICS in the first week of June, 1944, prevented the Germans from knowing the area chosen for the long awaited Second Front. The Nazi High Command thought that several diversionary landings would probably take place on the Dutch and Belgian coasts, in Normandy and in south west France while the main thrust would be in the Pas de Calais.

Two days before D-day the meteorological forecast indicated rough weather until June 8th or 9th which led the Germans to suppose that no invasion in any of the likely areas could be expected for four or five days. Despite the weather, General Eisenhower, as Allied Commander-in-Chief, embarked his British, Canadian and American forces on the evening of June 5th to arrive off the Normandy beaches in the early hours of June 6th. In Jersey, Guernsey and Sark people could hardly fail to realise that some gigantic military operation was afoot. All night long wave after wave of planes flew over the islands towards the French mainland. Peter Frampton of Jersey was at a friend's hotel in Archirondel on the evening of June 5th.

> There was this big drone which came up to quite a crescendo as the planes came near. There must have been hundreds, probably thousands as well as gliders going over. Then the German ack-ack batteries all over the island opened up. They let rip with everything they had and the ground really shook. We thought – this is it. The battle of Normandy is about to begin.

Entries in Leslie Sinel's *Occupation Diary* also describe the armada of planes passing over on the night of June 5th and into the following morning.

96

The Germans in the Channel Islands, thinking that the Allies would soon arrive, began an anti-invasion routine. A proclamation was issued warning people of the death penalty if they attacked German forces or committed acts of sabotage. Red Cross flags went up on hospitals in Jersey and Guernsey and guards were doubled at the labour camps.

Dr. John Lewis of Jersey was so excited at the prospect of the Occupation coming to an end that he felt quite unable to go to bed. Instead, he took a mattress and a blanket outside on his lawn and spent the night listening to the miraculous sound of what he felt sure was the Second Front. Next morning the BBC news confirmed that the Allies had landed in France. Hopes for an early release were widespread among islanders but even when Montgomery had captured Caen and Falaise and the Americans had reached the Loire Valley there was still no sign of liberation. Yet Marcella Darling of Jersey, like thousands of others, believed that rescue must soon come from the armies in Normandy.

We looked across and we could hear the gunfire because British naval vessels were bombarding the French coast not far away – a distance of about fourteen or fifteen miles. And the sound of it was very, very loud. So we thought any day now they'll be with us.

Two months after D-Day Alexander Coutanche, the Bailiff of Jersey, and John Leale, President of the Controlling Committee in Guernsey, realised that liberation was not likely to come for some time. They also realised that, as no food supplies could now come in from France, grave shortages could be expected in the months ahead. There was little in the news to promise a swift victory for the Allies. It was not until August 25th that the last Germans in Paris surrendered to the Americans and the French Resistance led by the Free French force of General Leclerc. As the tanks of the liberators rolled through the streets tens of thousands of Parisians, in an eruption of joy and thanksgiving, swarmed round them, offering wine, food, flowers and kisses. On September 4th Brussels fell to the British and Canadians but the end of the war was still nine months away.

People in the Channel Islands reacted in different ways to the period of waiting – an anti-climax after the first emotions of excitement at the time of the June landings on the Normandy beaches. Schoolboys who had grown up during the Occupation were now young men in their late teens. There were fewer in Guernsey than in Jersey because very large numbers of Guernsey children had been evacuated to England before the Germans arrived. In the autumn of 1944 a number of young Jerseymen, bored with the restrictions of daily life and fired with a youthful bravado, made attempts to escape by sea to France with the idea of joining the British Army and fighting the Germans.

Among the many youngsters taking a chance at escaping in small boats was the young Peter Crill, one day to be Bailiff of Jersey, then aged nineteen, and two of his friends, Roy Mourant and John Floyd. Peter Crill remembers that the weather was rough when they decided to go.

The summer of 1944 was fairly stormy. There were problems on D-Day and the storms carried on intermittently through the autumn. We were ready to go. We had the outboard motor ready and we had the petrol which we had siphoned from German lorries. I suppose you would call that stealing today but I'm afraid we looked at it slightly differently then. We'd also hoarded some provisions. It was a question of waiting until the time was right. Then we got a tip off that there was going to be a couple days of fog and flat, calm weather. So we went.

The first problem was to get away from the beach without the Germans spotting us. We knew that they always did their patrols at regular hours, like clockwork. Every night at eight-fifteen they would leave the beach and go into the hut for supper and to play cards. They would remain shut in until a quarter past ten. So we had at least two hours to get clear.

There was another boat leaving at the same time – a much larger boat which also had an outboard motor. We didn't use the motors at first in order not to make a noise but rowed some distance out to sea. Outboard motors in those days were pretty temperamental. If they got wet they were the devil to start again. We started ours and it went all right but the motor in the other boat didn't start so we came alongside to throw them a tow-rope. Water came into our motor because the two boats were side by side and we shipped water when manoeuvring them. So our motor stopped. Whereupon, without another word, they hoisted their sail and disappeared.

A little further on we had two mishaps. We broke the compass and then we thought we'd anchor because it blew up a bit. But we couldn't use the anchor because the rope was tangled. That probably saved us, in a sense. If we had anchored we'd probably have been caught. So we decided to carry on. We hoisted our sail and I steered by the wind. If the wind had changed we'd have gone round in a circle. But fortunately it remained north-west and, by keeping the wind in my left ear, we went more or less straight towards France.

At the place where we came ashore there wasn't anyone in sight. So we dragged the boat up and went on to find a local bistro. Inside, one of the men said – which way did you come? We pointed to where we had left tracks in the sand. And they said – you're very lucky because just that part of the beach hasn't yet been cleared of mines.

A total of fifty-nine escapees left various Jersey beaches to attempt the crossing to France. Six were drowned on the way. Six had to turn back and were shot or imprisoned by the Germans and forty-seven arrived safely on the French coast. In addition, there had been an attempt by Dennis Vibert of Jersey during the first six months of the Occupation. He tried a second time, rowing most of the way towards England because his outboard motor had ceased to function and finally coming to within a few miles of Portland where a Royal Navy destroyer picked him up. Brought ashore by the Navy, he volunteered at once for the RAF.

Those who set out for France from the Jersey beach of Fauvic had the help of the Bertrams – two families who lived nearby and did everything from concealing boats to supplying hot drinks for fortifying the youngsters at the start of their voyages. Bill Bertram was awarded the British Empire

Medal after the war. Other teenagers who did not sail for France expressed their ardent and restless feelings in different ways. Joe Mière, formerly the curator of the German Military Underground Hospital in Jersey, was sixteen in 1944. He joined others of his age in scrawling swastikas on the houses of people suspected of collaboration. They also wrote V-signs on walls. The German secret police considered these acts to be insulting to the *Führer* and they arrested the boys, including Joe Mière.

They took me down to their headquarters and they left me in a cell for about an hour. I thought at first – this can't be too bad. They'd been polite enough – very correct in their manner. All of a sudden I was invited into this interrogation room. They said - would you mind coming? As soon as you got in the door you had a fist in the face and another in the stomach. Before you know where you are, you're on the floor spitting blood. They take you back to the main prison in the early hours of the morning. Then next day they don't want you but the day after they come and get you at about two o'clock in the morning.

You go by car and they put you in a cell with a straw mattress. You think if you keep still and don't make any noise they'll forget about you. All of a sudden you're invited into the interrogation room and the treatment starts all over again. – politeness, offered a cigarette, offered a cup of acorn ersatz coffee and before you know where you are you're on the floor again and there's somebody kicking you.

So, eventually, they couldn't get any truth out of us after weeks and weeks of this so we're marched through the Parade gardens, up along Rouge Bouillon to the court martial. It was a bit of a comedy. There was a German colonel with a monocle who was president of the court. And behind him was a picture of Hitler. They give you only a lance-corporal to defend you. When that's over they march you back to the prison, with a couple of Germans behind you with Tommy guns in case you make a bolt for it. You look back on things like that and you say – that's life. C'est la vie. I put it down to experience.

By November food stocks and other supplies in the Islands were almost exhausted. Estimates showed that, within a month or six weeks, the civil populations would face starvation. The German garrisons, too, were on short rations. The total isolation of the area now that the Allies controlled the French coast had implications well understood by the Bailiffs of Jersey and Guernsey. At the end of August, only three months after D-Day, Alexander Coutanche of Jersey had already demanded from his agricultural officer a statement of the food stock position. The Bailiff of Guernsey, Victor Carey, had also ordered a statement from Raymond Falla of the Controlling Committee. Finally, both Bailiffs produced their separate memoranda, duly signed and addressed to the International Red Cross in Switzerland. The Germans agreed to forward them. It was in their interests to evade responsibility for feeding the Island populations.

The Jersey Bailiff, Alexander Coutanche, had given a second copy of his memorandum to one of the young men escaping to France, Norman Rumball, who was going to send it to the Home Office in London. From Guernsey the list of foodstuffs and supplies went to London by way of Fred Noyen, a retired sea captain who had become a Guernsey fisherman. He had made a plan with his friend, Bill Enticott, to evade the German marine guards and get away to England. Everything went smoothly and they landed in Poole fourteen hours later.

Important items in the Guernsey and Jersey communications revealed the position as follows.

All rations drastically reduced.
Bread finishes 15th December.
Sugar finishes 6th January.
Butter finishes end of December.
Hospital anaesthetics, if used sparingly,
may last until mid-January.
Essential drugs now exhausted.
No gas since September.
Electricity will finish end of year.
Footwear and textiles almost finished.

It was the coldest Christmas in living memory. The Resident Medical Officer at the hospital remembers that Casualty Department dealt with numerous cases of chopped fingers caused by people taking axes to furniture and floorboards to get wood for warming their houses. Elderly people living on near-starvation rations died from the cold. Jennie Seymour of Jersey lived through those December days of 1944.

> *One thing that sticks in my mind was being so hungry. It hurts when you're really hungry. My mother had given me a small piece of swede – raw swede. I remember eating it and, at the same time, feeling guilty because I knew it was the next day's food.*

In the ranks of the German Army in the Islands hundreds of men wanted to get out of the war. Low rations, monotony and a sense of defeat spread disaffection in the garrisons. A mutiny was planned, as yet only in secret talks between the soldiers and whomever they could depend on for help among civilians. Norman Le Brocq of the Jersey Communists and his comrade, Les Huelin, had received a visit from a German soldier some months previously and gradually the details of the conspiracy developed, as Norman Le Brocq recalls.

> *We were able to produce leaflets for him as we had a duplicator, paper and stencils available – and we were pre-pared to duplicate his leaflets – which was all he wanted at that stage. And so that particular part of our work started, with me being appointed as liaison with the soldier - by name Paul Mullbach. I used to meet him at a place where we had a friend which we knew to be safe. It was a bookshop in the Parade and I used to rendezvous with Paul there from time to time. He would give me a manuscript text of a leaflet he wanted. We would then get it out on the duplicator in the number of copies required and I would return the package to him in the same shop.*

Preparations for the mutiny slowed down in the autumn and the soldier, Paul Mullbach, had by this time deserted and was given civilian clothes and other help by Norman Le Brocq and the Communists. As winter came in the shortage of food and unusually cold weather delayed the work of organising rebels in the garrisons.

Morale among the Islanders was also at a low ebb. Then, on the 27th December, a response from Switzerland and London arrived, showing that the various messages describing the condition of the siege had got through. The Red Cross ship, S.S. *Vega*, loaded with 100,000 food parcels from Canada and New Zealand, came into St. Peter Port and, a day later, into St. Helier.

Distribution of the food parcels among the Islanders met with no opposition from the Germans. Headquarters in Berlin had agreed officially that the Red Cross food was for Islanders only. It was a matter of military honour for local commanders to carry out the agreed terms. Yet rations for Germans were down to a bare minimum. A New Year's message to the troops from their Commander-in-Chief, von Schmettow, said that they must be ready for more sacrifices in 1945. It was important, he said, to maintain comradeship, self-discipline, faith in ultimate victory and the will to fight to the last.

A fortnight later von Schmettow issued an order that troops should do no more than five hours duty a day and must rest in bed for two hours in the afternoon. In this way their failing energies would be conserved for the defence of the Islands if the enemy should come.

At the end of February a fanatical Nazi, Vice-Admiral Friedrich Hüffmeier, took over command of the Islands. He at once ordered measures to stiffen the will to survive among the troops. A daily guard of honour would be mounted outside Staff Headquarters. He issued a special message for Heroes Day. When troops passed officers in the streets the Nazi salute had to be given with maximum smartness. There had to be no more fraternisation with local women. Stealing food would be punished by having the culprit's ration cut. In repeated cases the death penalty would apply.

Despite Hüffmeier's threats of punishment, stealing food went on. Sheer primitive hunger drove some soldiers to make raids on domestic pets. Cats and dogs disappeared from houses because they could be cooked into some sort of meat dish. Brian Read, now living in Henley-on-Thames, was then a youngster in Jersey and remembers the last winter of the Occupation.

> *The Germans could get very little food for themselves. There were rumours that they were stealing cats and dogs to eat. Until the 31st of March I didn't believe it but on that Saturday evening I was alone at home reading a book when I heard a neighbour shouting – "they've taken your cat". I was seventeen at the time and both my parents were out. But I dashed outside and was in time to see two German marines legging it towards the beach. By the time I reached them it was too late. They had cut the head from a much loved Persian cat and they were holding it up by its back legs with blood pouring on to the sand.*

German soldiers were going round the streets of St. Helier and St. Peter Port grey in the face from despair and hunger. They were so thin that uniforms hung on them like scarecrows. Leslie Sinel of Jersey said: "When they first came here they were the cream of the German Army, proud and vital. At the end they were old men poking about in dustbins for scraps of food." But Vice-Admiral Hüffmeier was resolved to defend the Islands for the Führer, cost what it may. At a meeting in a St. Helier cinema he told the troops: "I shall hold out with you here until final victory."

The soldiers were not interested in victory. They wanted the war to end and plans for the mutiny were almost ready. Leaflets circulated among the non-commissioned ranks, the leaflets composed by Paul Mullbach's circle of conspirators and printed on the duplicator of Norman Le Brocq's friends. Hüffmeier knew that he was in danger of being assassinated. He moved from place to place as little as possible and then only with a bodyguard to shield him, not because he was afraid for his own skin but because he knew that he was the only commander capable of holding the Islands in these days of crisis. As von Schmettow had said a few months earlier, "The Germans do not build mighty fortifications without holding them to the bitter end."

In March and April of 1945 news came through on hidden radios describing the advance of the Allies on the western front. British and

104

Canadian forces were across the Rhine and fanning out over the plains of North Germany. A Polish division was at the Ems estuary. To the south the Americans drove their tanks into Wiesbaden, Frankfurt and Mannheim while the Free French occupied Baden-Baden. On the other side of Germany, to the east, the Russians hurled their armour against the crumbling defences of Berlin. It was all over for the Nazis and Hitler committed suicide in his underground bunker while shells from Russian guns exploded outside.

In the Channel Islands the last days of the Occupation brought the certainty of liberation ever nearer. Shops were already selling Union Jacks on May 1st. On May 2nd a portrait of Winston Churchill fetched 400 Reichmarks at an auction. On May 3rd a young German shot himself in a lavatory in the Jersey Hospital. The next day the banks were besieged by people trying to get rid of German money. On May 6th men in the secret police, fearing mob violence, put on army uniforms and mingled with the troops. The news on 7th May was that the war in Europe would end within twenty-four hours. On May 8th wireless sets were tuned in to London for Winston Churchill's speech announcing the end of the war. In St. Helier loudspeakers carried the broadcast to a vast crowd in the Royal Square.

It was a solemn moment when the voice of the Prime Minister came on the radio. He said: "Hostilities will end officially at one minute past midnight, tonight, Tuesday, the 8th May but in the interests of saving lives the cease-fire began yesterday, to be sounded all along the fronts - and our dear Channel Islands are also to be freed today."

The Bailiff, Alexander Coutanche, stood on the balcony of the Royal Court in Jersey and, facing the crowd in the square, led the singing of "God Save The King." In Guernsey, too, scenes of great emotion followed the broadcast and that night a victory bonfire sent flames into the sky above the cliffs of Sark.

CHAPTER 9

Liberation and Aftermath

THE SURRENDER OF GERMAN FORCES in the Channel Islands was not so straightforward as it might have been if the Commander had been anyone else but Vice-Admiral Hüffmeier. He was not a man to accept defeat. Four days before the historic cease-fire Southern Command of the British Army sent a radio message to Hüffmeier suggesting that he should make clear whether he intended offering resistance to the liberating force, bearing in mind that the end of the war was near. No reply came through until three days later. It was terse and to the point. "I only take orders from my government."

On May 7th the Germans in Europe capitulated to the Allies and the Nazi Admiral Dönitz who had inherited Hitler's authority sent a radio signal to Hüffmeier, ordering him to surrender. An order from a superior officer, particularly the Supreme Commander, was not a communication to be ignored. Yet Hüffmeier was disinclined to obey. He had always said that he would hold out in the Islands whatever happened on the other fronts. He believed that his troops could be kept alive for months solely on Jersey and Guernsey milk when other food stocks had ended. Moreover he was in command of the most strongly fortified positions in western Europe.

It was in a spirit of compromise that he radioed British Army Southern Command fixing a rendezvous near Les Hanois lighthouse off the south west corner of Guernsey. In answer to the message, Brigadier A. E. Snow, in charge of the liberation troops, left Plymouth in the destroyer *H.M.S. Bulldog*, accompanied by *H.M.S. Beagle*. Arriving at the rendezvous, he expected to meet Vice-Admiral Hüffmeier in person but, instead, a rusty minesweeper came out to the lighthouse bearing a junior officer who said he was authorised by his chief to discuss terms for an armistice – that is, a short cessation of hostilities.

Brigadier Snow at once set the record straight. There could be no armistice. Hüffmeier or a properly accredited deputy must sign a document certifying the unconditional surrender of the Islands. But the confrontation was not yet finished. The junior officer replied that, if the armistice discussion was not acceptable, *H.M.S. Bulldog* with Brigadier Snow had better depart from Guernsey waters otherwise they could be fired on from the shore.

To this deliberate misunderstanding of the situation Brigadier Snow responded with admirable British aplomb. He told the young German officer to go back to his master and tell him that if he persisted in this attitude he would certainly be hanged after the Islands had finally been brought under a normal administration. Ten hours later another emissary from Hüffmeier appeared, Major-General Heine, the Island commander of Guernsey. Hüffmeier had evidently thought over his predicament and realised that either he would have to obey the order from the German High Command or, if he continued to hold out in the Islands, would do so in complete isolation.

It was midnight when Major-General Heine came aboard to discuss details of the hand over. At 7.14 am. the following morning he signed six copies of the surrender papers. Six more were signed by the local commander in Jersey and the Occupation was officially at an end.

An advance party of two hundred British troops came ashore in St. Peter Port and received a rapturous welcome. Another two hundred, arriving in St. Helier, were also greeted with cheers, flag waving and demonstrations of joy. Union Jacks flew from masts and flagpoles and hung over balconies and windowsills. To add to the atmosphere of festival the RAF put on an air display and sent Mosquitos and Mustangs roaring over the Islands. As for Sark, the commander of the first contingent of troops could not spare any men to take the Island over. Instead, he delegated his authority to *La Dame*, Sybil Hathaway, who relished once again being in charge of her domain. She immediately put her Germans to work clearing mines.

After the Liberation scenes and the church services of thanksgiving a long repressed explosion of fury erupted against women who had been too friendly with the Germans. Many were girls, aged about twenty. They had done no more than follow their normal instincts with the only young men available but crowds in the St. Helier streets gave them a rough treatment, including head shaving. A group of self appointed avengers tried to throw one of the girls into the harbour but some men nearby stopped them at the last moment.

The notorious Ginger Lou, the super courtesan in French shoes, was a special case. She had done well for herself in clothes, luxuries and food. Some said she had given away the names of people who had radio sets in their homes. When the Germans at last left the Island she went into hiding in a house in St. Helier but after a few days she must have become bored with her captivity and she came out for a walk and was recognised in Seaton Place. In no time at all a hostile crowd surrounded her - mainly women whose hatred had been smouldering through all the years of the Occupation. They were about to lynch her from a lamp-post when some British soldiers saw what was happening and came to the rescue.

The food shortage profiteers of the black market were in another category which qualified for revenge if they could be found and identified. There were also the informers, those anonymous people with grievances, paying off old scores by giving information to the German police about anyone infringing regulations. Usually the informers acted from mere stupidity without understanding the consequences. The person informing on Louisa Gould who gave shelter to an escaping Russian slave, probably had no idea of the long journey from the court martial to prison, followed by transportation to Germany and finally to eventual death in a gas chamber at Ravensbruck concentration camp. Informers were difficult to name although many were suspected. Most of them remain unknown to this day.

Reorganising life in the Islands after the liberation presented a variety of problems, not only to the States but to officials from Whitehall who arrived to report on what was needed to put the Islands on their feet again. Trade had to be restored and the ownership of shops and property established. German money collected by the banks was now valueless. The British Government redeemed the Reichmarks with a gift of seven million pounds. A large scale clearing operation began on the mines left by the Germans, 67,000 in Jersey and just under 50,000 in Guernsey.

Sark lived through this time in its own special way. Memories of the Occupation did not have the same bitter taste which characterised events in the larger Islands but Sarkees had had their troubles. The deportations had taken away Miss Ducket and Miss Page, owners of the Dixcart Hotel, Mrs. Pittard, a widow, and Robert Hathaway, the husband of the Dame of Sark. Shortages of clothes had beset the Islanders as in Jersey and Guernsey but, in a small community, Sarkees could more easily make exchanges and, in a general way, support each other. Sybil Hathaway turned one of her rooms at the *Seigneurie* into a workshop where jackets and other garments were made out of curtains and any other materials brought in.

The easy tolerance between Sarkees and Germans favoured a relaxed atmosphere which made daily life less irksome, despite the war and the Occupation. But the Commando raids did much to upset this cosy situation without, as in Guernsey, achieving results of immediate military use. One unexpected item of information did come to light. The Commandos took away a copy of the *Guernsey Evening Press* which happened to be the issue containing the deportation notice and was the means of conveying this news to Whitehall.

Among the occupying forces in Sark was a young medical orderly named Werner Rang. He formed a romantic friendship with Phyllis Baker, the daughter of a Sark farmer. Phyllis had attended the German classes at the *Seigneurie* and had learned to speak the language quite well. She was much in demand as an interpreter when the local German Army doctor had to examine his Sark patients for he was the only medical practitioner in the Island.

One day Phyllis Baker fell ill herself, staying for a day or two in bed. Werner Rang happened to be the orderly who brought the doctor's pills to her house but, as he knew no English, he was unable to make himself understood by Mrs. Baker at the door. Phyllis called to her mother from above, telling her to send the young man up. It was the beginning of a serious relationship. After the war when Werner Rang finally left the prisoner of war camp in England he married Phyllis Baker and they settled down in Sark to live out their lives together. The main sentimental event in Sybil Hathaway's Island had a positive and wholesome flavour somewhat more pleasing than the unfortunate liaisons in Jersey and Guernsey.

In Alderney at the time of the liberation none of the original residents were there except Frank Osselton and the Popes. The Island was mainly populated by the Germans who maintained it as a defence position covering the waters to the west of the Cherbourg peninsular. It was also the site of four German camps - three for workers on the fortifications and the fourth a concentration camp for political prisoners. Investigations after the war revealed that the number of prisoners and workers was 4000 in 1943, falling to 245 a year later when the fortifications were completed. Most of the concentration camp prisoners died from their privations. It is said that many were executed before the arrival of the liberation force.

The Army garrison (as distinct from the S.S.) must have been quite large for so small an island. 2,332 German prisoners of war left Alderney for camps in England and 500 remained behind to clear up the mines, the barbed wire and other residues of military occupation. In Hitler's dream of the island fortresses Alderney would have had a strategic importance, commanding as it does the sea lanes of the Channel and the western approaches of the Atlantic.

People coming back to Alderney after the war and finding the damage done to their houses and belongings blamed Judge French for suggesting an evacuation in the first place, forgetting that he had given them the choice and received their votes of approval. Seeing Frank Osselton and the Popes installed on their farms, the returning exiles felt that they need not have gone away.

The homecoming in Jersey and Guernsey was also marred by inevitable difficulties of adjustment to the new conditions of 1945. There were those returning who had been in England for five years, including many children without their mothers for, particularly in Guernsey, some parents had sent their children away for safety and now the children came back as strangers, grown up and speaking in the unfamiliar accents of Manchester and Glasgow. Young men had gone away to join the army or one of the other services and some had been killed in action. Others returned with wounds and disabilities.

Islanders who stayed and the others who went away could not understand each other. Their personal experiences during the five long years had been utterly different. Those who had stayed in the Islands accused the evacuees of running away. The people coming back from England accused the other Islanders of having too much comfort at home and being too friendly with the Germans while England was fighting the war.

There were those who had been in German internment camps, among them Ambrose Sherwill and Frank Stroobant of Guernsey and many others. Some of the men and women from the prisons and concentration camps came back - those who had survived such as Bill Symes of the Fountain pub in St. Peter Port and Stanley Green of Jersey who had photographed lists of the Island fortifications prepared by a retired army officer, Major Crawford-Morrison. The roll call includes Charles Machon, Frank Falla and their helpers in Guernsey, heroes of the G.U.N.S. underground press, two of whom never came back. They died, like Canon Cohu of Jersey, from malnutrition, the freezing winter cold and prison brutality.

A brief mention of names does insufficient justice to the martyrs of the Occupation. In the case of Louisa Gould, her name and her death in a concentration camp are inscribed on the war memorial of St. Ouen in Jersey. Harold Le Druillenec should be on the list of those arrested by the Germans, later to experience the horrors of the camps. A task yet to be undertaken in Guernsey is the compilation of a complete roll of honour. A list of names of the Jersey resistance exists in the St. Helier Town Hall, with copies at the German Underground hospital and inside the Cenotaph

Living at close quarters with the Germans created human relationships that were at times perplexing. The Germans were the enemy and yet they often showed an unexpected friendliness. Charles Duret Aubin, Jersey's Attorney General, was on friendly terms with his opposite number, Baron von Aufsess, finding him amusing and open in his opinions. It was von Aufsess who saved Ambrose Sherwill's wife and children from deportation at the risk of his own execution. Louis Guillemette, secretary to the President of the Guernsey Controlling Committee, formed a friendship with a German official because they were both organists and music made a common bond.

After the war German Army officers were mostly unemployed, many of them living on charity. It was not until five years later that the Federal Government of West Germany was able to offer pensions. Some people in the Islands sent gifts to make life easier. Arthur Harrison of the *Jersey Evening Post* had been working throughout the Occupation with a German officer who censored the paper. This man after the war was in reduced circumstances. His wife was ill and expecting a baby. Arthur Harrison sent him a food parcel. Ambrose Sherwill, on a visit to Germany, came upon

111

Major Bandelow, the officer who had been helpful in the case of Symes and Nicolle. He was working as a groundsman. Sherwill sent him money.

Another gesture which emerged in the post-liberation period was a collection of money among the Islanders. They had not forgotten the food parcels which had saved them from starvation in the last winter of the war and they contributed a total of £170,000 to the International Red Cross.

The Germans who gave their countrymen a bad reputation were those in the S.S. – the *Shutzstaffel*, Hitler's elite corps. A one time resident of Sark, Major Breen, had been Press Attaché at the British Embassy in Berlin before the war. He met Himmler, the Head of the S.S., and asked him why German prisons and concentration camps were staffed by sadists and perverts. Himmler replied that it was the best way of using them - to crush opposition. In contrast the German Army had a tradition and a code of honour. It disliked the methods of the S.S. Ambrose Sherwill who had dealt with all sorts of Germans, first as President of the Guernsey Controlling Committee and then in the internment camp at Laufen, said that on the whole he had received courtesy, consideration and kindness from the Army and one example of outstanding chivalry. His three months of solitary confinement in the Paris prison which was run by the S.S. did not encourage similar thoughts.

It is because the Channel Islands were small, self-contained communities that the inhabitants had to find individual ways of adapting to the Germans in their midst. In those days the island communities, including the Germans, represented on a small scale the problems and frustrations of the larger territories outside. A strange assortment of characters played out the drama. Human qualities came sharply into focus. Among the Germans and among the Islanders there were the good and the bad. The upheaval brought out the courage and strengths of some as much as the frailties and greed of others, both on the German and on the civilian side.

This was a cross section of humanity, of people surviving in the close confines of a community at war. It is over fifty years since the Germans came and now the Occupation seems like another age, a strange interlude in the memories of those still living in the little world of the Channel Islands.

*Left: Observation tower –
Naval coastal artillery.*

*Below: Anti-tank
traps at L'Etacq,
Jersey.*

AUFRUF

AN DIE BEVOELKERUNG DER INSEL JERSEY

Der Feind Deutschlands steht im Begriff, französischen Boden anzugreifen.

Ich erwarte von der Bevölkerung der Insel Jersey, dass sie unbedingt ruhig bleibt und auch bei Uebergreifen des Kampfes auf die Insel sich jeder feindlichen Haltung und Sabotage gegenüber der deutschen Wehrmacht enthält.

Bei Auftreten der geringsten Anzeichen von Unruhen werde ich die Strassen für jeden Verkehr sperren und Geiseln festnehmen lassen.

Angriffe auf die Wehrmacht werden mit dem Tode bestraft.

Der Kommandant der Festung Jersey,

HEINE,
Jersey, den 6. Juni 1944. Oberst.

PROCLAMATION

TO THE POPULATION OF THE ISLE OF JERSEY

Germany's enemy is on the point of attacking French soil.

I expect the population of Jersey to keep its head, to remain calm, and to refrain from any acts of sabotage and from hostile acts against the German Forces, even should the fighting spread to Jersey.

At the first signs of unrest or trouble I will close the streets to every traffic and will secure hostages.

Attacks against the German Forces will be punished by death.

Der Kommandant der Festung Jersey,

(Signed) HEINE,
Oberst.

D-Day precautions, 1944.

Above: St. Peter Port Harbour. Armed cargo vessel for carrying supplies between France and the Islands.

*Centre and below:
Checking the
Mirus Battery,
Guernsey.*

Above: Cleaning barrel of an SKL/45 at Noirmont Point, Jersey.
Below: Inspection in Sark. Admiral Hüffmeier (centre R.)

Above: Target practice in Alderney.
Below: Action Stations in St. Helier Harbour.

Testing fire power. Above: Grouville; Below: St. Ouens Bay.

*Above: Strongpoint –
Waiting for the
British to come.*

*Centre: Camouflaged
gun emplacement near
Mont Orgueil Castle,
Jersey.*

*Below: Covering
the breakwater at
St. Catherine's.*

Above: D-Day alert.

Right: Pets as food – starvation period.

Above: Red Cross ship Vega *delivering food parcels.*
Below: Going home with stocks for the larder.

Above: Liberation ships, St. Peter Port (Herm and Jethou in the back-ground.) Below: On board HMS Dulldog, Major-General Heine, Guernsey Commander, presents his credentials before negotiating surrender terms.

Above: First British arrive.
Below: Portrait of the Liberators.

Above: The Pomme d'Or Hotel, St, Helier, German Naval Headquarters.
Below: Union Jack replacing Swastika at the Pomme d'Or.

Above: Liberation Day scene.
Below: Listening to the Churchill victory speech through loudspeakers.

Above: German Army, Navy and Air Force prepare to leave.
Below: Germans on their way to prisoners-of-war camps in England.

Part 2

The Background

CHAPTER 10

Storm Warnings

HISTORIANS LOOKING BACK to the nineteen thirties would see the indecisions and false steps which led year by year and inexorably to the Second World War. Political parties were urging different policies in France and Britain, the two countries which might have prevented the rise of Nazi Germany. There were voices in the Westminster parliament calling for a curb on German rearmament but their opponents believed that Hitler should be allowed some latitude as it looked as if he would provide a useful bulwark against the spread of Soviet Communism.

In France the Socialists of the *Front Populaire* urged the nation to resist Hitler as each crisis brought new threats to international stability. They preferred Russian Communism to German Fascism whereas in Britain the Socialist Left was not so strong. Officials of the French Quai d'Orsay and those of the Foreign Office in London were unable to follow a common line in decisive moments when the course of history could have been changed.

The first opportunity came in 1934 when Hitler sent his troops into the Rhineland, a neutral area guaranteed by treaty as a *cordon sanitaire* between France and her long standing Germanic enemy which had twice invaded French territory since the Franco-Prussian war of 1870. At the end of the Great War of 1914 the three triumphant allies – France, Britain and the United States – had Germany on its knees, defeated, ruined and compelled to accept the conditions of the Treaty of Versailles which would, it was thought, prevent the German nation from ever arming again to disturb the peace of Europe.

It was this treaty which Hitler flouted when his forces went into the Rhineland in 1934. The French would have stopped him at once by military intervention but the British hesitated and allowed Hitler the advantage of a strategic move on the chessboard of diplomatic politics. Soon afterwards

German armament factories in the Ruhr were turning out guns and tanks in contravention of this same treaty. For the second time a concerted effort by Britain and France could have stopped the drift towards war.

Winston Churchill, then a back bencher, warned the House of Commons and the Government that a resurgence of German militarism was in the making. But leading members of the cabinet - Halifax, Simon, Baldwin and, later, Chamberlain – favoured appeasement of the Nazi regime, supported by Geoffrey Dawson, editor of The Times, and others in the so-called Cliveden set, still hoping that Hitler would stand in the way of the red tide of Communism.

Other influences, too, may have kept the Government on its fatal course. To sanction a large scale manufacture of armaments in Britain for the Army, Navy and Air Force would have required increases in taxation which might have been quite unnecessary, the Government argued, in view of Hitler's declaration that he had no claims on territories in the west. So, if for no other reason, foreign policy seems to have been based on two factors – fear of Soviet Communism and a conviction that unpopular taxation would lose the Government the next election. Stanley Baldwin himself, in a moment of frankness, said so.

No one could say that the Channel Island States tried to avoid sharing defence expenses with the United Kingdom. Jersey and Guernsey jointly voted a contribution of £280,000, an impressive figure at the time. Apart from the financial gesture, they encouraged their young men at the outbreak of war to volunteer for the British armed forces and later introduced a law for conscription in order to bring the recruiting procedure in line with that of the United Kingdom.

But in Westminster new legislation was needed because of an historical proviso in the Channel Island constitutions. According to Royal Charters dating from the fourteenth century, able bodied men were exempt from military service outside the Islands unless required in special circumstances for the protection or rescue of the King of England. After the outbreak of war Jersey and Guernsey decided to waive this ancient constitutional right.

A difficulty now cropped up. The terms of enrolment in the Channel Islands differed from those set out on the United Kingdom entry form and the Home Office realised that a new law in parliament would be needed to rectify the discrepancy. A long delay ensued while Whitehall considered ways of overcoming the difficulty which, in fact, had originated in the War Office. Deliberations went on for so long that the matter was settled only two days before the Germans arrived in the Islands. In the meantime, young men in the local defence forces had volunteered and were already stationed in England.

The first stirrings of a realisation on the part of the Jersey and Guernsey States that the Islands might play a part in the United Kingdom defence arrangements arose in the mid-nineteen thirties when the British Civil Air Guard scheme came to the attention of the Bailiffs. This was a way, they thought, of preparing men for entry into the RAF on a voluntary basis and of associating the Islands with the mainstream of the British defence programme, as yet – it must be said – not clearly defined even in Whitehall.

Entry into the scheme involved purchasing light aircraft and subsidising flying clubs where prospective pilots could be trained. Both Jersey and Guernsey were eager to go ahead with these arrangements but the Air Ministry did not respond enthusiastically. It seemed reluctant to accept the Islands into its organisation on the grounds, the Ministry said, that it would prove too expensive for them, bearing in mind the relatively small numbers of potential recruits. Distance from England was also a discouraging factor.

The nineteen thirties drew to a close. Even after the declaration of war in 1939 the idea that the Germans would come to the Channel Islands was not a thought that anyone entertained as a serious possibility. The Lieutenant-Governor of Guernsey went so far as to tell the Bailiff that he might perhaps expect small raids from time to time and that Bofors guns or some other anti-aircraft weapon might be needed. A few infantry units might also be useful in the event of small enemy raiding parties landing on one or other of the beaches.

Nevertheless, the authorities discussed how to improve their local defence forces, usually known as the militia. This, they thought, would at least show that practical measures had been taken. But when the Guernsey States attempted to buy coastal defence guns from the United Kingdom they met with a forecast of long delays before the guns could be sent because of the priority given to War Office needs. The volume of weapons being produced was still less than the massive total of Hitler's armaments.

The months went past and suddenly the war fronts burst open in the spring of 1940, revealing the Channel Islands to be dangerously exposed in the new military situation. Messages flashed between the Islands and the Home Office and between the War Office and the Admiralty but a great deal of confusion arose from hastily improvised plans and a faulty co-ordination between one ministry and another. The Home Office believed that, in the last resort, the Army would protect the Islanders if the Germans came within shooting distance.

As a defence measure the War Office ordered the dispatch of a battalion of infantry to Jersey and another battalion to Guernsey. Winston Churchill's war cabinet agreed with this at first and then reversed its decision on receiving the next assessment of the situation from the Chief of the Imperial General Staff which concluded that, as the Germans had by now come close to the Normandy coast with a vastly superior force, the two battalions would be lost if sent to the Islands and, in any case, were much needed in England.

Meanwhile, men of the Machine Gun Training Unit, at this time located in Alderney, were to move to Guernsey and Jersey to replace Naval ratings who had been guarding the airports. The Admiralty then told the two Lieutenant-Governors that the airports were no longer required for the Fleet Air Arm and could be closed and all flying aids on the ground put out of action. A copy of this communication did not reach the Air Ministry which issued a contrary instruction to keep the airports open and guarded for use by the RAF.

It was in this changing situation that the Jersey and Guernsey Bailiffs with their Lieutenant-Governors wanted to know if and how the Islands could be defended. Throughout the first two weeks of June, 1940, when the Germans were sweeping all before them the War Office was considering whether the Channel Islands should be demilitarized – that is, whether to order the withdrawal of all remaining Military, Naval and Air Force personnel and issue a declaration to that effect so that the enemy would cease to regard the Islands as a military target.

By mid-June the Chiefs of Staff had decided that demilitarization was the only sensible course but they continued to delay the announcement, merely saying that demilitarization was a possibility. This silence caused the Island authorities a great deal of anxiety. Alexander Coutanche, the Jersey bailiff, recounts in his memoirs how the prevailing uncertainty made him take matters into his own hands. Aided by the Lieutenant-Governor, he pressed the Home Office to give him precise information on what was being planned.

The Home Office in response summoned him to London for a conference on the subject. He made ready to depart. A small aircraft belonging to Channel Island Airways stood by to fly him over. Clearance for the flight from RAF Fighter Command did not come through until the next day and, in the meantime, a crisis had erupted. Coutanche had to stay in Jersey to organise yachts and other rescue boats for the evacuation of British troops stranded in St. Malo. In his place Jurat Edgar Dorey flew to London.

Dorey's discussions at the Home Office elicited the news that demilitarization would take place. It was unfortunate, even tragic, that this information was not given to the Germans until it was too late to prevent an air attack on the Islands which killed a number of people and injured others. Next on the agenda was the question of evacuating the Island populations to England. How many people would want to go? Ships could be provided, the Home Office said, if a few days could be allowed for organising the operation.

On his return Jurat Dorey went first to Guernsey to report and then went back to Jersey. He told the States that English residents would probably decide to leave, either in the evacuation ships or by making their own arrangements. As for Jersey-born people of Norman origin, he thought they should stay behind in their native Island. He was particularly harsh on them and said, in a dramatic moment in his speech, that if any of those who had roots in the soil of Jersey were to leave he would consider them to be rats and rabbits.

Plans for the evacuation were soon in hand for those outside Jurat Dorey's category of people who should stay. In Guernsey, too, the authorities made preparations for the embarkations and awaited the arrival of the ships. Escape to mainland Britain seemed to offer a deliverance from the Germans whom people thought of as an advancing horde of barbarians. They had heard of the Gestapo and the concentration camps. Telephone lines to the United Kingdom were overloaded with calls from residents and others trying to contact friends and relations. Panic ran like a contagious disease among those undecided whether to stay or go. At the last moment for the embarkations people in the country parishes of both Guernsey and Jersey made such a desperate exit from their houses that they left doors open, the beds unmade and, in at least one case, with a half finished meal on the table.

Coutanche in Jersey and Sherwill in Guernsey endeavoured to keep their people calm and they discouraged those who were not in the priority categories from leaving. Of the two men Coutanche was the more successful, largely as a result of his many public speeches in which he said that he and his wife would remain in the Island. It was a more difficult task for Sherwill in Guernsey who was not, in any case, the Bailiff with all the authority of that office.

Among those going away were some who buried their personal possessions and valuables in their gardens. But some had paper assets deposited in banks. What was to be done with bonds and securities lying in tin boxes lodged in bank strong rooms? If the documents were to fall into the hands of the enemy they would be as good as lost. The Germans could sell them in many markets in Europe and America as it would be impossible to prevent transactions on the international exchange.

A desperate race against time followed. The banks decided to send all their records to London before the expected invasion. Bank officials worked night and day to complete the documentation and to pack bond and share certificates into sacks. Nearly a hundred of these bundles went out of the Islands in the last days before air and sea connections with England were severed.

The Home Office had already discussed the banking system in Jersey and Guernsey because it realised that day to day commerce in anything like normal conditions would need support for local currencies. The decision arrived at was that banks should remain open in the Islands, maintain if possible their level of business with whatever staffs they still had and that Bank of England support would be available when hostilities were over. It was thus implied that liberation from the Germans would come in the end.

In the meantime the enemy had still not heard of the demilitarization of the Islands. It afterwards became known that the War Office had not wanted the information released because it might have encouraged the enemy to invade the Islands immediately. The Home Office, with an admirable concern for the safety of the communities, gave an announcement to the press but this, too, was withheld for the same reason.

It was at this time that the King's letter went to the Bailiffs. The Home Office added a note that the contents which included the demilitarization decision should be made known to the Islanders. This meant that Home Office officials hoped that the Germans would hear about it through their intelligence services. The effort to please the War Office and the Bailiffs was almost bound to be useless. A misplaced caution by all concerned led to the air raid on June 28th and a needless loss of life. Three days later the Germans landed.

CHAPTER 11

The Sinews of Government

THE ARRIVAL OF THE FIRST CONTINGENTS of the German Army in that summer of 1940 created two different sets of problems. There were, first of all, problems for the Islanders in having to live with the newcomers and all their new demands. A second set of problems confronted the Germans. Accounts of the Occupation tend to emphasise the predicament of the civilian populations and how people adapted to their subjection under a foreign army. Yet the invaders had to adapt as well. They were in what was for them enemy territory and in the midst of people who had good reasons for being hostile, the newcomers having taken over private houses and hotels for living quarters and offices and then imposed unwelcome restrictions such as the curfew.

It was clear to the German Command that ways of co-existing with the local populations and of meeting their basic needs had to be found if the occupation were to proceed without multiplying the inevitable difficulties. This meant, in the first months at least, treating civilians carefully and encouraging their co-operation. The Germans turned their attention first to the utilities – gas, water and electricity. They realised that these services would run more smoothly if the personnel were left in place. Thus a working relationship with a few groups of Islanders began. They also needed the help of the Island authorities for transmitting regulations to the public and for maintaining some degree of civic organisation. Senior officials in the two bailiwicks were right in deciding to accede to German demands of this kind so that some semblance of ordinary day-to-day living could continue.

The relatively benign rule of the invaders during the first year arose partly from a propaganda line which claimed that as the Islands were originally French the Germans should be considered as liberators of the people from the colonial grasp of the British. This was Hitler's over-simplified way of formulating geo-politics. Another reason why the Germans took care at first to avoid a too blatant appearance of tyranny was to prepare themselves for dealing with the English in what they believed was to be their imminent conquest of Britain.

When Colonel von Schmettow (soon to be General) was appointed Commander-in-Chief of military forces in the Channel Islands his superior officer said to him: "Remember you are going to English territory, not to defeated France." With that in mind, von Schmettow instructed his officers to treat the Islanders with respect and consideration.

The official line coming from the top ranks in Berlin reveals a contradiction in German thinking. On the one hand it suggested that the Channel Islands were a part of France and that, on the other, the inhabitants were British and that the invasion of the Islands was, in a sense, a rehearsal for the occupation of Britain. In addition, some members of the top personnel in Jersey and Guernsey had a liberal point of view when it came to governing the local populations. Colonel von Schmettow was a soldier of the old school imbued with a tradition of military honour. Another of the senior officers, Baron von Aufsess, was an aristocratic landowner who understood his responsibilities and his obligations to everyone who depended on him. Major Lanz was a scholar with interests in the arts and philosophy. As for German soldiers in the ranks they showed the same basic human tendencies as soldiers everywhere. They could be led into the savagery of conflict but, left to themselves, they faced life with a cheerful good humour.

Explanations such as these do not absolve all those concerned in the Nazi programme of expansion over Europe but they have relevance to an assessment of relationships during the Occupation.

Civilian leaders in the two bailiwicks, Ambrose Sherwill as Head of Affairs in Guernsey (deputising for an ailing Bailiff) and Alexander Coutanche as Bailiff of Jersey both saw that the enemy was likely to be amenable to manipulation if each of them could keep his nerve. It was nothing short of a disaster that Ambrose Sherwill was so soon to be overwhelmed by the ill-fated expeditions of spies and commandos in Guernsey. Alexander Coutanche in Jersey did not have to meet eventualities of that sort. He was able to preserve formal relations with the Germans and was thus in a position to challenge their edicts and regulations from time to time. When, after the war, a press interviewer asked him what he had done during the Occupation, he replied: "I protested."

As a lawyer by profession, Coutanche knew how to make protests and to present a legal case. A game of bluff and diplomacy began. It was a question of which authorities, German or Channel Island, could play the right cards. Coutanche and Sherwill (in his time) aimed at avoiding useless clashes with the Germans. What they wanted for the Islands was a measure of justice, enough food to ensure a reasonable level of good health for everybody and as much freedom for the people as they could get under the new regime until their final restoration to Britain.

The Germans had some of these considerations in mind. They, too, wanted to avoid unnecessary conflicts with the people. The question of good health was likewise important. If food shortages were to weaken the Island populations infectious diseases might break out and spread among the German troops. Thus the aims of the occupied and the occupiers were to some extent the same. Meanwhile, Coutanche and Sherwill sought ways of obtaining the best advantage from the situation.

So long as the Island authorities made their demands firmly and protested over those orders which could reasonably be revoked they stood some chance of achieving their aims over ordinary matters such as indiscriminate rationing. No diplomatic representations could have prevented Hitler's deportation of English born residents in the crisis of 1942 but, in general, the Island authorities knew that the Germans could not do without them and this was their strong card.

If they tried to overplay their hands they soon found themselves up against a hard reality. By 1941 the Occupation had entered a new phase, less benign than the early months. The *Geheime Feldpolizei* (the Army secret police) which had been supervising security among the troops was now watching civilians, reinforced by Gestapo types in plain clothes. The top administration at the headquarters of the *Feldkommandantur* in Paris ordered that a firm hand must be shown to local governments in the Islands. Relations with the inhabitants, said the order, must not be too friendly, otherwise the populations might become difficult to manage.

Many people in the two main Islands worked for the invaders simply because they were keeping essential services going. If they had objected the

Germans would either have compelled them to continue working at the point of a gun or would have brought in their own technicians to run the electricity works, the sewage system and other municipal utilities.

The administration of the Islands came under an organisation called the Military Government which had its regional centre in St. Lo and its headquarters on the borders of Paris. As the Channel Islands were considered to be a part of France they were in the administration which covered other parts of Normandy. Instructions on all matters of food distribution, law and order, police and items of German policy came through the local *Feldkommandant*. The Islanders soon realised that behind the edicts of the States was a branch of the Military Government.

In his conquest of other nations Hitler relied on two state ministries, each with a different function. First of all, the *Wehrmacht* (Army, Navy and Air Force) carried out defence and combat operations. In 1940 it had reduced the armed forces of neighbouring countries to the point of surrender. It was when the peoples of these territories had been overcome that Hitler employed a permanent team of administrators including police to organise the life of the inhabitants and exploit the material resources of the area. This was the Military Government, the *Feldkommandantur*. One branch of it arrived in the Channel Islands a month after the invasion.

The States of Guernsey and Jersey continued to pass laws on minor matters but even these had to be confirmed by *Kommandantur* headquarters in France. In addition to regulations emanating from the Military Government, the *Wehrmacht* issued orders relating to defence. With so many new rules and instructions from different sources it was not surprising that people sometimes broke the regulations accidentally, apart from those they deliberately contravened.

Compromises had to be made when a clash of interests arose between the States and the *Feldkommandantur*. The jurisdiction of the courts was one point of disagreement, aggravated by the fact that, apart from the local court, there were the various courts of the occupiers. It was important for Islanders to establish their rights in those courts which ought to be their own. For instance, the military authorities were apt to claim prosecution priority if any army vehicle was involved in a road accident. The civilian culprit might have to appear in a German court as well as in the ordinary magistrates court.

139

When it came to crimes or misdemeanours which did not easily fit into one or other of the recognised categories the offender might have to be tried in any one of five different courts - the magistrate's court, the German Army court, the Navy court, the Air Force court or the *Feldkommandant's* court if the case had arisen from an arrest by the *Geheime Feldpolizei*, a department which came under the Military Government.

Offences against food rationing were a frequent source of trouble. Being out in the streets or lanes at curfew time was also an indictable offence. The *Feldkommandant's* court dealt with anyone attempting to escape from the Islands by sea. This applied particularly to fishermen. At first the Germans fixed a maximum limit to fishing as a mile from the shore or two miles with a guard in the boat or an escort vessel if there were several boats. Later on the authorities became nervous at the possibility of escapees taking away information about the fortifications and they banned fishing altogether. It was later restored but under increased surveillance.

The Germans always had in mind their need of certain key members of the communities for running the Islands, including the farmers. Yet they interfered in the work of producing food, especially in Guernsey. Before the Occupation tomatoes and flowers had been the principal export to England. Now, with the disappearance of that market, horticulture had to undergo a basic change. Greenhouses were to be used for food crops. Officials of the *Feldkommandantur* came to the growers to explain German methods of intensive cultivation. This was not the best way of developing good relations with people who had for hundreds of years been using the land to the best advantage.

A major problem facing both the Islanders and the Germans was how to produce enough food to meet their joint demands. The Germans at first thought that they could import substantial quantities of wheat, oats, flour and other agricultural products from France in order to supplement locally grown supplies but, as it turned out, their mainland organisation could not provide the required quantities. Finally, they authorised the Islanders themselves to set up a buying organisation in France. Thus the Germans came to depend even more on the people they had brought forcibly into their system.

To this end the States of Jersey and Guernsey set up what was called the

Channel Islands Purchasing Commission with a team of experienced men, including John Jouault from Jersey and Raymond Falla from Guernsey, among others. They made deals with Normandy and Brittany farmers and arranged the transport of produce back to the Islands. The operation was largely directed by Guernsey's Raymond Falla, an agriculturist, business man and all-round improvisator. These were the qualifications needed for wheedling and bargaining on the French side of the water.

Fuel was another basic material in short supply now that coal was no longer coming from the United Kingdom and so the Germans issued new regulations restricting household levels of heating. It was essential to assure sufficient quantities of coal for the gasworks and oil for the electricity company but such was the demand for electricity and gas for the ever-growing German forces in the Islands that householders received diminishing amounts from these sources for their heating and cooking.

The whole fabric of day-to-day living passed from the former free trade system to the centralised control of the Military Government. The *Feldkommandant's* place in the new organisation was that of a dictator. His orders were final. He requisitioned cars and bicycles to satisfy the occupier's need for additional transport. At the same time he had the authority to grant permission to certain essential people such as doctors or farmers to retain their cars or lorries. It was inevitable that, with the many regulations and overlapping spheres of influence, both occupiers and occupied should find numerous reasons for dispute. Yet each had to learn to live with the other because, as the Germans said, they would be in the Islands for a very long time to come.

CHAPTER 12

Food and Health

THE PRESENCE IN THE ISLANDS of German soldiers and other personnel in numbers which steadily increased as the Occupation proceeded demanded additional efforts to assure food supplies over and above those made by Raymond Falla and his team in France. Not only were there more people to feed but wheat, oats, dairy products and meat were available only in fluctuating quantities according to changes in the war situation. Flour for bread baking was a basic necessity, as the Germans realised. They recruited elderly retired millers to run the old mills – out of action for decades but now brought back for the emergency.

Maintaining a fair standard of health in the populations was a matter of concern not only to local medical practitioners but also to doctors in the German Army. They observed the effect of food rationing on the general condition of people to detect any signs of a serious run down of health. Some local doctors saw an improvement in persons who had previously been overweight. In Jersey Dr. John Lewis said that sparse rations seemed to have produced a good effect on some of his patients. They were healthier after losing excess weight. But persistent low rations could be serious, especially in cold weather.

After the Liberation the Chief Medical Officer of the U.K. Ministry of Health, on a fact finding mission to the Islands, noted that children's teeth were exceptionally sound. He attributed this to the lack of sugar and sweets during the five years of the Occupation. On the other hand, the children's body growth had been retarded by the reduced diet. Those up to fourteen years of age proved to be on average two and a half inches less in height compared with standard measurements.

Elderly people were less able to maintain a good condition on the meagre food supplies available and were also affected by lack of fuel for heating.

Everyone went through a period of great privation before the Red Cross parcels arrived and in the barren weeks when the extra food had been exhausted.

A fair estimate of the situation came from Frederick Brown, a retired Jersey civil servant. He thought that middle aged people – those up to the age of fifty or sixty - seemed reasonably healthy. "What I remember," he said, "was being hungry. Sometimes the rations were pretty low and we had to find ways of adding something. My wife and I used to go out of town on our bicycles to visit a farmer we knew of. After some bargaining over the prices, he would sell us perhaps two eggs and half a pint of milk. Of course, we ran the risk of being arrested if we were stopped on the way back or if someone in the *Kommandant's* office got to know about it. The farmer would have been in trouble, too. But a lot of people were doing it. It was a regular thing at weekends or when you had a day off. People in the town would make these excursions to see what they could get from their friends or anyone else in the country because that was where these extras were - on the farms."

Bicycles were essential on these occasions when a farm might be five or six miles out of town. A serious problem arose a year or so after the start of the Occupation. Bicycle tyres disappeared from the shops and could only be obtained by making a personal swap with someone who had one and needed something else in exchange. If it was not possible to get a tyre in this way, people wound rope round the rims of the wheels but this made a bumpy and exhausting ride.

The extra produce, whether it was from one of the farms or from the ration, still had to be cooked and the electricity and gas supplies were on tap at certain times only - one hour in the morning, one hour at lunchtime and one hour in the evening. As substitutes for normal heating there were burnable substances of various kinds, including sawdust in a paint tin. When slightly damp it burned for a considerable time. Some people took casserole dishes to their nearest baker for simmering overnight in the oven alongside his loaves.

If, as it seems, good health was often a compensation for eating and drinking less, it nevertheless required a sustaining minimum. The Islanders lacked even this when the first shortages came in the later months of 1941.

Saved-up tinned food had run out and these hoarded stores had until then supplemented the rations. People had not yet invented substitutes.

Frank Stroobant of Guernsey who ran the *Home From Home* café facing St. Peter Port harbour devised various dishes and concoctions before he was carried off to a camp in Germany at the time of the great deportations of September, 1942. His *ersatz* fish cakes made from minced limpets and parsnips were much in demand as were his swede rissoles. Raspberries later came on the menu, doused with a so-called 'cream' which was at first made with a combination of ice-cream powder, powdered milk and soya bean flour. The taste of the 'cream' improved later when it had only one ingredient – powdered milk in a thick consistency.

A favourite item in the café, considered a delicacy at that time by the clientele, was a plate of chips. Chips were hard to come by in those days because of the scarcity of cooking oil. When Frank Stroobant ran out of it he had to find a substitute. His first experiment used a little olive oil from the small stock he still had and this was mixed with liquid paraffin to make it go further. These ingredients, too, became unobtainable and he then tried frying with linseed oil but the fumes were so unpleasant in the kitchen and even penetrated the café that some absorbent was essential. At first onions served quite well and also improved the flavour. But as he had soon to economise on the onions he floated small pieces of wood in the oil as smell absorbers. Frank Stroobant was winning his battle of the shortages.

Stories coming out of Jersey had a different slant. They were mainly about getting round the regulations and deceiving the Germans. Donald Le Gallais, the baker of St. Ouen, remembers the case of two unregistered pigs that a farmer was hiding: "One day when I was out on my bread round," he said, "the farmer said to me – Don, quick, can you help me? The Germans are checking and they're just up the road. So I opened my van and said – if you hurry up and get some buckets and straw to put over their heads that'll stop them making a noise and I'll take them with me. We just managed to get one of the pigs into the van in time. I came back an hour later to find that the other one had been taken by the Germans. The farmer said – not to worry. I shall kill this one and give you a nice piece of pork."

Donald Le Gallais' wife, Ada, also carried out risky deceptions, as when she was helping a Russian fugitive on one occasion.

"Our house was close to one of the camps," she said, "and we often used to get those prisoners calling in and looking for food. And of course it became one of the first houses to get searched. One day there was a young prisoner with me in the wash house and I was just going to give him something to eat when a neighbour called out that there were Germans looking round quite close. Quickly I managed to get the young man into my copper where I usually had laundry boiling away. Fortunately it was empty and I put the cover over him. As the Germans approached the house I lit the faggots underneath and pretended to be busy with my washing. They walked in and saw what they thought was me doing the laundry and walked out again. If they had hung around things would have got a bit warm for the man inside the copper."

Food supplies in reasonably balanced varieties and fuel for home heating were basic for the general level of health. To these causes must be added the weather. Periods of storms followed by exceptionally cold conditions tested the Islanders' resilience in the last winter and were too much for some. In November, 1944, high winds swept in from the sea. In December the office of the *Feldkommandant* issued a warning that electricity supplies were likely to cease (which they did two weeks later). As an alternative could the populations depend on timber for heating?

The Jersey Department of Labour specified the amount of wood needed for fuel. Two thousand tons of logs or faggots would give each householder enough heating for a month. The Jersey General Hospital would require a hundred tons for a month. Another hundred tons was on the list for cooking and heating in special invalid cases.

In this freezing winter at the end of the Occupation people went to bed when it was dark and stayed under their blankets until daylight. The Leslie Sinel diary records the disappearance of all fuel at the end of January, 1945, after six weeks of intense cold and falls of snow. As the days lengthened, February brought in milder weather. Then the March period of chilly winds at last gave way to a burst of spring sunshine in the first week of April with temperatures up to 74 degrees.

But winter does not willingly loosen its grip and, on the 30th April, it returned to more cold and snow as if it wanted to match the last ditch stand of the German Commander-in-Chief, Vice-Admiral Hüffmeier. Both Hüffmeier and the winter had, in the end, to go and the Islanders were then on their way to regaining their normal vitality and average standard of health.

CHAPTER 13

Bargaining and Compromise

IN THE EARLY DAYS of the Occupation German soldiers walked around the streets of St. Helier and St. Peter Port as if they were tourists. To some local people they looked like the annual summer visitors who happened to be dressed up in military kit. Islanders who had face-to-face dealings with the Germans in the ordinary course of business, such as the Jersey and Guernsey harbourmasters, were inclined to view them as clients with a habit of making aggressive demands - as if the customer is always right.

As time went by attitudes changed. This was quite soon in Guernsey where landings by British spies and commandos upset the precarious balance of Occupation arrangements between the German and the Island authorities. Six months passed. Then a year. By this time the uniformed tourists had ceased to look like temporary visitors and had become what they really were - masters of this isolated corner of what was now the German Reich.

And yet the feeling of being holiday visitors persisted in varying degrees among officers and men of the German forces. Many years later some of them recalled their time in the Occupation for a programme made by Channel Television. Their enthusiasm for the beauty of the Islands was quite evident and also their surprising confidence in the friendly attitude of the inhabitants. Perhaps the passing years had clouded their memories or it may have been that they did not see what they did not wish to see.

It must be said that the men of the *Wehrmacht* had little contact with the seamy side of the Occupation. It was not the Army but the *Kommandantur* which dealt with civilians who infringed the regulations. Consequently imprisonment and deportation for crimes such as the possession of radio sets did not come to the notice of those members of the Army or Navy who found life in the Islands so enjoyable and welcoming.

A few people did make friendly overtures to the Germans at first. It is on record that a grower in Guernsey sent bunches of flowers to the Island military commander for the decoration of Government House, his headquarters. Another sent grapes. These two entrepreneurs evidently had future custom in mind and perhaps counted on a lenient attitude from the German authorities if troubles arose over the many new regulations. Whatever the explanation no one could regard these gestures as anything but a clear willingness to collaborate with the enemy.

Rumours of collaboration did for some years cast a lurid light on the activities of the Bailiff of Jersey and the Head of the Guernsey Controlling Committee, Ambrose Sherwill, and both men suffered from this. There were people who did not see that, in the absence of the British Army, the Island authorities had to bargain with the German administration for concessions.

With this consideration in mind, Coutanche and Sherwill issued instructions that there should be no resistance to the German occupiers. Everyone should keep calm and comply with whatever rules the newcomers imposed. This was an essential tactic, bereft as the Islanders were of military protection.

It seems highly improbable from all that is known of the Occupation that the leading men of the two bailiwicks were collaborators in the sense that they wished to assist the Germans in establishing a permanent Nazi administration in the Channel Islands.

The first suggestion of collaboration came as a result of a radio broadcast by Guernsey's President of the Controlling Committee, Ambrose Sherwill. The Germans had offered him facilities for making a recording which was to be sent to London in the expectation that the BBC would transmit it on the Home Service for listeners in the United Kingdom. Ambrose Sherwill's intention was to reach those Guernsey people who had gone away in the evacuation ships and reassure them that all was well with their relatives and friends who had stayed behind.

In the course of this radio speech Sherwill referred to the German occupiers as reasonable people who had treated the Islanders with courtesy and respect - which at that time was true. He made a point of saying that he was not speaking from a script written by the Germans nor did he have a gun pointing at him.

These comforting words did not reach the evacuees through the BBC which, after consulting the Ministry of Information, had every reason for withholding the recording. Softening up influences were not welcome when Britain was preparing for a German invasion and facing up to air attacks which were soon to escalate into the blitz. Winston Churchill was making his stirring speeches over the radio and saying that the British would fight in the streets, on the beaches and in the hills and would never surrender. It is not surprising that the BBC banned the broadcast. Sherwill's references to the gracious behaviour of the Germans seemed a little out of key with the prevailing mood.

But it was just what the Germans needed for their English transmission, backed by a commentary which contradicted stories of German atrocities - fabricated, they said, by Churchill's government. That the contrary view came from a leading personage in the Channel Islands was a bonus for the Nazis but Ambrose Sherwill's reputation was in shreds. It was only later that his name was finally restored after he had prevented the execution of Nicolle and Symes, two of the British officers who had landed in Guernsey as spies His arrest and imprisonment in Paris showed on which side his loyalties lay.

Gossip about the supposed collaboration of the Jersey and Guernsey authorities arose from suspicions that they were having secret talks with leading German officials. It was true that the authorities had frequent consultations with the *Kommandantur*. This was how they won concessions in matters affecting the welfare of civilians and, in more than one case, prevented the death penalty from being carried out on Islanders who got into trouble.

The Bailiff of Jersey intervened when two Frenchwomen, half Jewish, were arrested shortly after the D-Day landings in Normandy and taken to court for a crime against the Reich. It was a serious charge. The two women, with more patriotism than discretion, had typed out messages on slips of paper urging mutiny and passed them to German soldiers. Their execution would have followed if the Bailiff, Alexander Coutanche, had not made a personal plea to the Judge who turned out to be wise enough to see that executing the women was likely to cause other troubles. He converted the death penalty into life imprisonment - a term which lasted only a few months until the war was over.

Protests from the Island authorities brought into question all manner of incursions into their zones of influence which included infringements of the legitimate rights of conquered peoples according to the Hague Convention. There were protests when the *Kommandant* imposed a 20% reduction in the bread ration as a reprisal for RAF attacks on Germans shipping. In Jersey the Bailiff protested against the *Kommandant's* order that civilians should build a road to an army ammunition dump and also against the requisition of food stocks which had been imported from France by the Islanders themselves. All such arguments and discussions were effective only because of relations with the Germans fostered by the authorities in Jersey and Guernsey.

In France the position was more clear cut. The limits of collaboration were easier to define. On the one hand, men and women of the resistance movement risked their lives in the sabotage of German installations. On the other hand, French collaborators were clearly on the side of the enemy and helped to impose the new regime on the population. In between these two extremes were those who tried to carry on their daily lives by dodging the system where they could and complying or even collaborating, in small matters when they had to.

A significant difference in the Islanders' position in relation to the Germans was that resistance could not have lasted more than a week. The Islands were too small for an aggressive campaign of sabotage. There was no space to manoeuvre or to create safe hiding places. In France the men of the *Maquis* had the refuge of the mountains and the long distances of French terrain for escape. They appeared out of nowhere, tore up railway lines and disappeared into the night like ghosts. Escapades of this kind were impossible in Jersey or Guernsey.

The Islanders were in virtual prisons of a few square miles of land surrounded by sea. Alexander Coutanche, Ambrose Sherwill and others had to find ways of guiding their people through the hard years to the time of liberation. They were on their own. They had to make up their own rules. But at least there were guide-lines and these defined more than anything else the roles they were to play.

In Jersey the guide-line came in the form of a telephone call to Alexander Coutanche in the last hours before the Germans landed. The voice at the other end of the line was that of Sir Alexander Maxwell, Under-Secretary of State at the Home Office. His words to Coutanche were precise: "'It is the King's wish that you and the Bailiff of Guernsey remain at your posts. He will not accept the position of not being represented in the Islands at their moment of danger. You are carrying out the direct wish of the Sovereign. We know that we can rely upon you to face up to the situation, terrible as it may be. There is no advice that one can give to anybody in these conditions. But when we meet again I feel sure that I shall be able to say to you that you have worthily followed the example of Burgomaster Max of Brussels."

The allusion to the Mayor of Brussels was not lost on Coutanche who remembered the incident in the Great War of 1914. It is recorded that a German officer came into the Burgomaster's office and threatened him with a revolver. The Burgomaster replied by throwing his pen on the table and saying: "That is all I have to fight with."

That event in a previous war bears a resemblance to Ambrose Sherwill's surrender of Guernsey when he put his medals on the table and said that there were no longer any rifles in the Island.

Sherwill was to go through many troubles and changes in the next few years, experiencing solitary confinement in a Paris prison and deportation to a hostage camp in Germany. But he later spoke of his admiration for a top ranking German officer (Baron von Aufsess) who had saved his wife and children from deportation – a chivalrous act by the German which, if discovered by the Nazi authorities, would have meant his arrest and execution by firing squad.

Incidents such as this showed that the Germans and the Islanders were often closer to each other than the over-simplified picture of Huns against their victims. They lived together in the confines of the war situation and sometimes developed personal relationships quite different from the conventional categories of patriots and enemy.

When the dead bodies of British sailors from the torpedoed Royal Navy ship *Charybdis* were washed ashore in Jersey and Guernsey the Germans organised a solemn military funeral for their dead enemies, allowing Union Jacks to cover the coffins. It was, in its way, a salute to the human qualities of those caught up in the maelstrom of war.

Dealing with personal problems from day to day was the only course open to Channel Islanders caught as they were in the grip of the Nazi system. The question they asked themselves was how to hold fast to a faith that one day the war would end and liberate them from Hitler's regime which no one, not even some of the Germans, believed could stand against the combined military forces of the Allies.

CHAPTER 14

Hitler's Island Projects

THE HIGH COMMAND IN BERLIN pivoted on Hitler himself who nevertheless received advice from the General Staff, Jodl, Keitel, Dönitz and their aides. Although the advice was often disregarded in favour of Hitler's intuitions, it was obvious to all concerned that the *Wehrmacht* would have to gain control of the Channel Islands which, if left unoccupied, might provide bases for the RAF and the lighter craft of the Royal Navy, thus posing a threat to German forces already massing along the Channel coasts for the invasion of England.

From Hitler's point of view the Islands would have to be neutralised until the invasion had been accomplished. They might also have a practical use as supply areas for the German landings in South West England. But with the postponement of the invasion Hitler began to see that the occupation of the Islands would represent a diplomatic triumph, an early sign of Britain's Germanisation.

Soon the much vaunted landings in England, known as Operation Sealion, lost their priority in the Nazi timetable because of aircraft losses in the battles with the RAF. In the meantime, German forces had taken over the Channel Islands and Hitler became increasingly anxious to make them secure, believing that the British were awaiting a suitable opportunity to regain possession of them. They would be particularly vulnerable at times when his attention was directed elsewhere, such as when dealing with the Balkans or, later, when his forces were to cross the border into Russia.

He therefore gave orders to fortify Jersey, Guernsey and Alderney with sufficient armament and troops to resist possible landings by the British. The construction of defences and the allocation of additional *Wehrmacht* personnel therefore went ahead.

For the next twelve months the amount of building materials and armaments arriving in the Islands convinced some senior Army commanders that Hitler had taken an interest in these offshore areas far and away beyond their military worth. Alongside the engineering construction work supervised by Dr. Fritz Todt, the number and variety of guns ferried in was enough in the end to arm several fortresses which, in fact, the Islands were and it was thus that Hitler named them.

The fortifications may not have been as excessive as they at first seemed. Richard Mayne, the Occupation historian, writes that a glance at the nearby coast of Normandy shows that the range and number of the larger guns could supply artillery cover of the seaways from Cherbourg to Cap Fréhel, obviating the need for scores of batteries on the French mainland.

The largest guns in Guernsey, known as the *Mirus* battery, were reconditioned battleship guns. They were useful for the purpose they had in the centre of the Channel Islands, being capable of sending a 500 pound shell over a distance of 24 miles. In Jersey four 22 centimetre French guns were the largest. In addition, an artillery network extended like a ring of steel round the Island, with batteries at Westmount, Blanchepierre, La Haule, St. Aubin, Noirmont, Red Houses, La Pulente, St. Ouen's Church, Les Landes and round to the East in St. Martin, at La Coupe, Verclut and on to Grouville and Maufant. For use in case of attack by sea or from the air the Germans possessed numerous flak and mobile anti-tank guns.

Father Bourde de la Rogerie, of La Société Guernsiaise, and Miss Kathleen Nowlan translated the text of *We Defended Normandy* by General Speidel, one time Chief of Staff to Field Marshall Rommel. The book shows that Hitler had an eight year plan for massive fortifications in the Channel Islands. It was a project which obsessed him, perhaps for psychological reasons which went beyond military considerations. By the spring of 1944 the Islands had thirty eight strong points, concrete underground shelters for command posts and networks of tunnels for the storage of ammunition and vehicles.

General Speidel makes an astonishing comparison with Hitler's fortifications which extended from Dieppe to St. Nazaire. This coastline of 1000 kilometres (625 miles) had the same number of heavy batteries as the Channel Islands and only thirty seven strong points. A whole division of troops was stationed in Jersey and Guernsey, plus an anti-aircraft battalion and a tank battalion. Rommel recommended withdrawing a large proportion of these men who could be used to more advantage on the Continent. After the Allied landings in Normandy he begged the *Führer* to let him have the troops as reinforcements but was refused. Hitler's intelligence reports suggested – wrongly, as it turned out – that the British were about to attack the Channel Islands with a force approximating to a division. Rommel again pleaded for more men without success. At the end of the war the entire garrisons of both Islands had to surrender without having fired a shot.

Those who may think that the German chain of command proceeded from year to year without disagreements, without friction and according to an especially German logic would be surprised to learn that few military or administrative changes were what those in top positions expected. Developments came about after compromises between what the *Führer* demanded and what the Ministries and the officials of the Military Government could arrange. The result was often a confusion of half realised plans and much waste of manpower and equipment.

OKW in Berlin (*Oberkommando Wehrmacht* – the High Command) decided in 1942 to send a certain Major Lamy on a fact finding mission to the Channel Islands. He came to the conclusion, after looking round, that the number of personnel in the garrisons and in the *Kommandantur* was greatly in excess of normal requirements in a relatively small outpost of Hitler's empire. Most of the activities of the *Kommandantur* could well be undertaken by the Army, he suggested, as officers and men had little to do in the uneventful years of 1942, 1943 and up to June 1944. Major Lamy wanted to reduce the drain in men and equipment for what he saw as an unnecessary deployment of German resources.

These ideas did not receive a sympathetic hearing among senior officers in the Islands. They were on the whole competent military men but it would have been natural if they disliked the prospect of ending their pleasant sojourn in Jersey and Guernsey as a result of the rationalisation of duties and systems of administration. Nor did the military commanders wish to see their armaments down-graded in the overall evaluation.

Conflicts between individuals and the departments concerned had the effect of keeping things as they were. Major Lamy's sweeping reforms had little chance against the complications of German bureaucracy. Disagreements about the fortifications and manning of the Islands were symptomatic of larger problems elsewhere in the Nazi organisation. They marked a split between Hitler's inner circle of yes-men and the more practical members of the traditional officer class.

The split widened as the years went past. It showed itself in the suitcase bomb placed in Hitler's East Prussia headquarters when the Führer narrowly escaped death and it led to the subsequent Night of the Generals when all those disenchanted with Hitler's conduct of the war fell into the grip of the Gestapo, to endure an ignominious execution as traitors.

Revolts in the German Army, fanned by catastrophic losses on the Russian front, increased the disagreements over the fortifications and excessive manpower in the Channel Islands, symbolic as they were of the whole faulted edifice of the Nazi regime.

CHAPTER 15

Moves Behind The Scenes

THE LAST ELEVEN MONTHS of the Occupation were to change personal attitudes, both on the side of the Islanders and on the part of the Germans. There had always been a difference between reactions in Guernsey and those in Jersey. John Leale, President of the Guernsey Controlling Committee (replacing Ambrose Sherwill after the latter's arrest by the Nazis) respected the best among the Germans and he once said that it was important that the Germans should have a good opinion of the Guernsey people.

Members of the German forces returning after the war as tourists found no hostility in the Island which they had brought into the Nazi system. In at least two cases, they had married young women in the bailiwick and when released from prisoner of war camps in England, had settled down with their Channel Island wives and been accepted into the community.

It was different in Jersey where most people did not show the same tolerance, possibly because they followed the lead of the Bailiff who preserved formal relations with the occupiers and, unlike John Leale in Guernsey, did not concern himself with their good opinion or otherwise.

Guernsey people were perhaps more human and less ambitious than their fellow Channel Islanders across the water in Jersey. But in both bailiwicks the trials and tribulations of the last months of the war brought the inhabitants down to basic levels of survival, soldiers and civilians alike.

From the summer of 1944 the problem of supplying food to the Islands was uppermost in the minds of the Germans and the Island authorities. If the French ports of the Cotentin peninsular and as far round as St.Malo became isolated by the Allied advance in Normandy, German ships would be unable to reach the Islands with supplies. This meant that accumulated rations still in stock and whatever could be expected from the local harvests would have to feed the populations and the military garrisons in the months ahead.

The German Commander-in-Chief of the west, *Oberbefelshaber* von Kluge, realised that the Channel Islands might fall to the Allies, not in battle but as a result of starvation. He recommended that civilians should be transported to France or Germany so that food supplies destined for Jersey and Guernsey could be used exclusively by the *Wehrmacht*.

A decision one way or the other rested as usual with Hitler but it was so fraught with imponderables that he was quite unable to make up his mind on the question of mass deportations. The difficulty of providing ships was another problem. In July of 1944 the seaway from the Channel Islands to St. Malo was still open but Hitler's indecisions went on for so long that in the end this route to France was closed. As a result, lack of food and fuel was to undermine the morale of the garrisons in the last six months of the Occupation. The Islanders were fortunate in not being sent to join their English-born neighbours in camps on the Continent where conditions would have been rigorous in the extreme.

In October a calculation by the Commander-in-Chief of the Islands showed that civilians would be without food from the beginning of the new year. The Head of the Civil Affairs branch of the Military Government in Jersey, Baron von Aufsess, foresaw the supply problem as early as August, 1944, when the port of St. Malo fell into American hands. He composed a statement on the situation for his superiors which he intended for transmission to the British. It ran, after translation, as follows.

From 31st January, 1945, supplies for the civilian population can no longer be guaranteed. There is no question of a voluntary surrender of the Islands before Germany is defeated. We therefore challenge you (the British) to battle. If you will not accept the challenge, ships with supplies for the civilian population must be sent under the conditions set out below. Otherwise the civilian population will face starvation.

The wording of the text was especially designed to persuade the British Government to agree to send the food ships while, at the same time, conforming with the German Army's concept of its soldierly honour.

In the meantime the Bailiff of Jersey, Alexander Coutanche, sent a memorandum to von Aufsess in the name of the States, emphasising the

157

conduct after the war before the higher authority of the nations concerned. Baron von Aufsess in his Occupation Diary mentions this memorandum and says of Coutanche: "He is our sworn opponent....a wily old lawyer."

Appeals for food went through several channels to the British Government and to the International Red Cross in Switzerland. No one now knows which of these approaches was in the end decisive. There was the Guernsey statement of the position carried to England by the redoubtable Captain Noyen, sailing away at night in a fishing boat. There was the version taken to France by Norman Rumball, one of the young men escaping from Jersey. Two other versions of the appeal went through official channels - the Bailiff of Guernsey's letter to the Red Cross in Switzerland and a copy of Coutanche's memorandum to Baron von Aufsess which went by way of the Swiss Embassy in Berlin.

An alternative proposal, based on von Kluge's plan, came from the Germans. This was an approach to the British Government, to be made through the Protecting Power (Switzerland), suggesting an evacuation of civilians from the Islands, excluding men of military age, with guaranteed free passage through the English Channel without interference from coastal guns or aircraft. After much discussion in Cabinet, Churchill came to see that the most practical solution was to send food through the Red Cross.

No military objections were voiced by the War Office whose opinion continued to be that the Channel Islands had no strategic importance. To whichever source the response can be credited, the fact is that the Red Cross cargo ship *Vega* arrived in the Islands at the end of December and this saved scores, even hundreds of lives.

This additional food which came from many parts of the Empire but notably from New Zealand and Canada consisted of tinned products such as spam, baked beans, milk powder, cereals, sugar and necessities like soap. It brought the daily diet per person up to 1137 calories but it showed that the new supply, though vital, was no more than a supplementary ration. A normal daily requirement would have been 3000 calories. The recipients were nevertheless grateful and overjoyed, even more so when a second Red Cross consignment arrived five weeks later.

The Commander-in Chief of the Islands, von Schmettow, was a man who acted according to traditional army codes when dealing with conquered peoples. His orders were that Red Cross parcels destined for the Islanders were not to be touched by the troops or any other members of the *Wehrmacht*. This attitude was adhered to even when German soldiers and sailors were so hungry that they went out scouring the beaches for limpets to eat.

Among the top officers three stand out as being particularly reasonable and scrupulous in administering German regulations – General von Schmettow, Colonel von Heldorf and Baron von Aufsess. But they had to act within the rules laid down by higher authorities, one of which was that, with the arrival of the Red Cross parcels, they were to take a large proportion of local grains, vegetables and dairy products for the garrisons. As a result the Islanders had not much more than their Red Cross parcels to live on.

The bleak winter of 1944 and the first months of 1945 was to be a time when human values were to be tested in both the Islanders and the Germans. It was a time when hunger and fear engendered an outlook of stark realism. This was the beginning of a new urge for the changes which were to come, for better or for worse, in the post war world.

CHAPTER 16

End-Game

IN THE LAST YEAR of the war the balance of power between the three services in Hitler's High Command shifted from the Army towards the Navy. One reason for this was Hitler's loss of confidence in senior military men after the suitcase bomb and the revolt of the Generals. The Navy on the other hand had always shown unswerving loyalty to the *Führer*. It was a change of emphasis which affected command circles in the Channel Islands.

A newcomer appeared on the scene in the summer of 1944 to take over the post of Chief of Staff, deputy to the Commander-in-Chief, von Schmettow. He was Vice-Admiral Friedrich Hüffmeier, much respected in the German Navy for a daring exploit in 1942 when he commanded the pocket battleship *Scharnhorst* and saved it, with its sister ship *Geneisenau*, from certain sinking by the Royal Navy. Being appointed as Chief of Staff in the Islands was a prelude to Hüffmeier's final move to the post of Commander-in-Chief in place of von Schmettow.

The officer supervising all territories in the area of the English Channel and the North Sea was *Oberbefehlshaber - West*. He foresaw that a sudden change from von Schmettow to Hüffmeier would cause trouble between the Army and Navy. For this reason Hüffmeier became at first von Schmettow's deputy, thus bringing a Naval influence to bear on policy decisions without alarming the Army.

Baron von Aufsess, as Head of Civil Affairs, observed what was happening. He notes in his Occupation Diary that, in the latter part of 1944, Hüffmeier seemed to be having more and more to say about what should be done. Electricity was being distributed too generously, Hüffmeier said, when it was needed for Naval dockyard repairs. Another of his suggestions was that rations for the troops were too high and that civilians should also have their rations reduced. At a later stage he said that civilians should be evacuated to the French mainland so that local supplies of food could go exclusively to the garrisons.

Meanwhile the transfer of power from Army to Navy was becoming more and more obvious. Alexander Coutanche in his memoirs recalls that at some time in this siege period von Aufsess told him that four people in the Island were under suspicion as being unreliable – von Schmettow, his Chief of Staff at the time, von Helldorf, von Aufsess himself and also the Jersey Bailiff, Coutanche. It would only be a question of time before all four were removed, von Aufsess said and added that a place had been reserved for Coutanche in the Alderney concentration camp.

In the early months of 1945 Hüffmeier told his naval chief at *Marine-oberkommando-West* that von Schmettow was failing to inspire his officers with the will to hold on to the Islands in the increasingly critical situation developing. The axe fell on March 1st when Hüffmeier was given overall command and von Schmettow received orders to return to Germany on the grounds of ill health. A court martial awaited von Helldorf for failing to carry out repressive measures on the Islanders. In fact, von Heldorf was a conscientious administrator and he had seen the advantage of treating the populations reasonably.

The administration of the Islands became more and more like a gothic melodrama. Officers lived in the midst of sinister whispers and rumours. They suspected each other of disloyalty to the *Führer* and of letting slip indiscreet remarks about brother officers. They had to guard their lips as if the slightest word might betray a treasonable thought which could lead to the gallows, a mode of execution reserved for traitors.

As for men in the non-commissioned ranks, they shared the feelings of the Islanders. Both groups wanted an end to the war and the Occupation. They were on a common level of misery as human beings. Only Hüffmeier and the younger officers imbued with Hitler's faith in the future believed in ultimate victory or saw the point of continuing the struggle.

The position of von Aufsess, a known lover of the English, was becoming increasingly perilous. Every day he expected his arrest and removal to Germany. A friend of his in the signals section promised to let him know if a telegram arrived. If this happened he would put into operation his plan of escape across the water to France where the American Army was now in control.

He knew three Jersey people - two men and a girl - who also wanted to leave. They owned a sailing yawl in Gorey harbour powered with two outboard motors. Von Aufsess provided petrol and rations and arranged with another friend, the officer in charge of the harbour, to let the boat put to sea when the time came. He provided himself with identity papers in the name of a French labourer in order to avoid being held by the American Army.

Ordinary German soldiers in the Islands already saw themselves as prisoners of war. Rumours went around of prison camps in Canada waiting to receive them. In the joking way that soldiers have in bad times, they called themselves the Canada regiment. Some were planning mutiny.

News came in daily of gigantic losses by the German Army fighting on its home front against the Russians in the east and the Allies in the west. Around the top officers in Hüffmeier's entourage the melodrama reached new heights of suspense. Von Aufsess knew that his escape could not long be delayed. But at the last moment, receiving a posting to Guernsey, he became separated from the owners of the boat in Gorey harbour and from his friend in the signals section.

By watching his every move he survived and, as days and weeks went by in March and April, he even gained Hüffmeier's confidence. Questions of loyalty were irrelevant after the arrival of the British liberation force in May when twenty-seven thousand Germans became prisoners of war and von Aufsess went with them to temporary captivity in England.

Throughout the years of the Occupation relationships between Germans and Islanders were sometimes on an ordinary human level distinct from official attitudes as when the German soldier in Guernsey took Charles Machon to a last meeting with his mother. Among the higher ranks, Major Lanz showed an intelligent understanding of people in his contacts with the Guernsey States. General von Schmettow handled those under his command, military personnel and civilians, with the outlook and values of an earlier generation. Above all others, people remember the sterling qualities of the Head of Civil Affairs in the Military Administration, Hans Max von Aufsess, a man of wide human sympathies and an experience of life which comprised all that was best in the European tradition.

Comparisons can be made between the German occupations of the

Channel Islands and other parts of Europe. It has been said that Jersey and Guernsey suffered less from the Nazi system than places on the Continent. In the words of one Jerseyman, it was a relatively benign occupation, harsh and tragic though it was for those languishing in hostage camps or others who fell into the hands of the SS in continental prisons.

Among the best of the German occupiers there was a real affection for the Islands with their old-fashioned way of life and their scenic beauties of valley, beach and rocky cove. To see the green *cotils* sloping towards the sea and the lush meadows with their farms after the hardships of the war fronts was like coming to paradise, one of the newcomers said.

When von Schmettow was based in Jersey at the beginning of the Occupation he had Cardington Lodge as his private residence and liked to take walks in the Noirmont woods. Von Aufsess, too, was charmed by the landscape and the sandy beaches where he loved to canter his horse. German ex-servicemen, interviewed after the war, said they were struck by the beauty of the Islands and many came back on holiday in later years to see their wartime billets and the gunsites where once they had kept guard on the cliffs and promontories.

In 1940 the Islanders looked on the Germans with suspicion and were hardly overjoyed at being taken over by uniformed foreigners. Even original Norman families felt themselves to be British with a fundamental allegiance to the Sovereign of England, their protector since medieval times. If, as often happened, German soldiers made attempts to be friendly, the Islanders were uncertain how to react. This was the tightrope they trod on all levels. The Jersey Bailiff and the President of the Guernsey Controlling Committee had to perform delicate balancing acts when negotiating concessions from the invaders.

The *Kommandantur* and the *Wehrmacht* held all the aces in this unequal game until the winter of 1944. Power was theirs to exert over men and women trying to carry on their daily lives. But, as the Occupation entered its last six months when siege conditions and food shortages affected both sides, a curious reversal of popular sentiment took place. Whereas in the early years the Germans had been the more confident of the two, a gradual lessening of their morale brought them nearer to the level of the populations. It was now the Islanders whose confidence grew with every passing day.

Everyone knew that the end of the war was in sight. For the Germans no glorious future lay ahead. A complete social and economic collapse in the Fatherland would follow in the wake of defeat. Half starved soldiers of the once proud German army began to look like bands of bedraggled scavengers. Leslie Sinel, in a later television interview, recalled the change and said he felt sorry for them. No one could have predicted that a time would come when a Jerseyman could say that he was sorry for the Germans.

After the war a return to the old way of life in the Islands was no longer possible. People had been through too much. There were demands for a new type of government. In 1948 the composition of the States Assemblies changed to give seats to elected members in place of the unelected jurats and parish rectors. It was an outward sign of the beginning of a new era. Much of the pre-war style of every day living was lost but the world itself was changing and the people in these offshore communities had to change with it.

Above: Another time. Another war.
Below: Photo call for summer visitors (Fortress Engineer Staff 14).

Left: Off-duty at St. Ouen's Manor, Jersey.

Below: In the garden of Feldkommandantur Officer's Mess, Jersey.

German military funeral of RAF Sergeants Butlin and Holden shot down over Jersey.

Above: German officers fraternising.

Centre: Soldiers recreation club, St. Helier.

Below: Interior with German nurses.

The enemy meets free enterprise.

German officers relaxing in the sun.

Austrian and Swiss receptionists compete with local girls.

The end of an era – prisoner officers disembarking in England.

PART 3

The Germans

CHAPTER 17

Close Up Of The Occupiers

MEN AND WOMEN in Jersey, Guernsey and Sark living through the war years from 1940 to 1945 looked at the German invaders and had their own thoughts about the strangers in their midst. To some the newcomers seemed at times friendly enough. To others the Germans wore the forbidding mask of intruders who took over the Islands and introduced regulations that, to say the least, were inconvenient. Some lived in fear of arrest and deportation to the concentration camps of Germany for using secret radios to receive the BBC news of the war.

Now that the Occupation has receded into the distant past people may ask what the Germans themselves thought of the Islanders whom many of them met almost daily. And what did the Germans think of the war and the strange fate which had brought them to these off-shore communities? A series of interviews carried out by Channel Television showed how they responded to the local populations and to their sojourn in the Islands.

The television team had the task of prompting the memories of men long since discharged from the German armed forces. Transcripts of the original interviews have been edited down to the following texts. Most are translations from the German. A few are in the English of those who had a good command of the language.

That the invaders were going to be harsh masters was very much in the minds of local people awaiting their arrival. Everyone had heard, through newspapers and the radio, of the bitter wind which had blown over Germany in the nineteen thirties, later sweeping the Jews and other victims into the prisons and concentration camps or into exile. It was therefore a surprise when the newcomers seemed, on the whole, to be reasonable and friendly.

The brutal SS in charge of camp prisons, the guards of the Todt Organization and the Field Police were all under separate authorities from the command structure governing officers and men in the Army, Navy and Air Force among whom we can recognise, in varying degrees, a normal reaction to life and human relationships.

They give an impression of wanting to reach a workable understanding with the civilians and a desire to be accepted on an ordinary social basis. One of them says that neither side wanted the war – not the Germans nor the Islanders. It is clear that the average soldier felt almost as much a victim of the situation as the people whom he had over-run.

Captain Hans Kegelmann had been in a tank battalion on the Russian front where he was wounded and placed among those sent back to the west in an exchange of personnel. He arrived in Jersey in the first part of 1944.

> *I had the good fortune to come to Jersey. I took over a company which at the time was stationed in the Aberfeldy Hotel and then we were transferred to Brabant in Trinity. I already knew something of the significance of the Channel Islands – and the historical reasons for them – about William the Duke of Normandy who was later the first King of England. Also I had some knowledge from school of the English language. We were a little bit favourably disposed towards the English - at home in Germany, too. There was a kind of – how can I put it – a kinship, and they were a bit closer to us simply on account of the language and on account of this kindred relationship which was caused by those royal dynasties.*
>
> *It felt almost like at home, I must say. The Jersey people were normal. They behaved normally. They were not afraid. They were in a relatively good situation, they were well dressed, they had beautiful houses, they had roads. In fact, they had everything they needed. There were water mains. Waste disposal was provided and there were many other things which we had at home, too. And so there was a perfect impression, as if there had been no war. It was like being on holiday.*

Hans Kegelmann seemed to develop an easy understanding with the few

Jersey people he met, particularly away from the town in the country parish of Trinity. When food stocks were low he had dealings with a farmer and bought eggs from time to time.

> *We had our turnips, too – those crops which were basically in large quantities but were monotonous. There were always people who kept us going. You might call it bartering, where we gave something and got something else in return. And so things were good. I must say, there were no agonies in this situation with the Jersey people. There was close co-operation in this sense – in a human sense – which is something outside of nationalities. And the quietness and peace in the island was wonderful. There were very few alarm days when planes entered the air space or enemy patrol boats appeared off the coasts. It was basically a good time here. Jersey was really a reserved zone which didn't have to suffer much of the horrors of war – apart from the restriction of convenience, the scarcity of food and petrol and diesel oil and so on. Of course, the people were occupied and they were under another power and naturally they couldn't do exactly what they wanted.*

When Channel Television asked him if he had heard of a resistance movement in Jersey he said he did not believe that such a thing could have existed.

> *Jersey is an island. There was no possibility of hiding and disappearing. It was easy for the occupying power to search everywhere. And another thing, the general situation was not so serious or so menacing for the Jersey people as it was in France. There was perhaps more a sense of national honour being taken away. Otherwise they had little to complain about. After all, no great dangers had come from the German occupation. Of course, they'd had enough of us. But war is war. They just had to make the best of it. I can't say I met with any resistance groups.*

Captain Kegelmann seems to have looked on the bright side of things and this was probably how most of the Germans saw the situation. Now, years later, they remember the easy-going way of life and they genuinely did not understand why the *Kommandantur* in Jersey and Guernsey arranged the deportations of 1942. Nor did they know of the arrests of those aiding the escapes of the Russian slave workers or of the martyrdom of Charles Machon and his team who ran the Underground News Service in Guernsey.

Another German who had pleasant memories of that time was Kurt Spangenburg, a sergeant in a machine gun battalion who arrived in Guernsey in 1940.

We were very impressed by how beautiful the Channel Island of Guernsey was – all well cared for like a beautiful garden. Also the people were English. Whether they were Guernsey people or Jersey people they were English to us. And we knew that England or Britain had a special association with the Channel Islands. They were the last possessions of Normandy which still belonged to Great Britain. So we made contact with the local cultural circle. Many soldiers said, after being in France, it's almost like at home, the people are friendly. You could understand English better than French and so the whole attitude of the Germans – it was very positive. Many Guernsey people were employed by us as lorry drivers or they were in the kitchen or they were in the officer's mess.

It was essentially different from France. You could move around freely. You weren't forced to carry weapons – that is, pistols. Only what was compulsory, a knife in a sheath. That was always so in the German armed forces in peace-time even. But otherwise you didn't need anything. As soon as you went to France you had to have either a pistol or you had to have a rifle on you because you had to expect to be shot by the Resistance.

We all thought the people in the Island were so clever and intelligent not to offer resistance which would only have been a disadvantage for them – more of a disadvantage for the civilian population than for the soldiers. For we say in German – pressure generates counter pressure. After curfew – eleven o'clock in summer – civilians would still be riding by on their bicycles and we could have stopped them and locked them up but we didn't think of it. They said gute nacht *and we said 'goodnight' too. And another thing – because the civilian population lived here the British never made a bombing attack. I always said the Channel Islands were the best air raid shelter in Europe.*

To come to the Islands in the early days of the Occupation was to experience them at their best. Werner Grosskopf was an NCO in command of a platoon. He remembered his first sight of the coast of Jersey as the ship drew near.

It was a wonderful day when we went over there – blue sky, wonderful sunshine. There was really an enthusiasm on the ship when we saw the harbour of St. Helier, the white villas and houses and the wonderful clear, blue sea. As we landed I was thinking back to my exchange as a pupil – going to England in nineteen twenty-nine to learn the ways of English life. So from the first day I always said to my soldiers – now we are in a country where milk and honey are flowing day and night.

My first impression of the population in town and also in the countryside was that they had been very much shocked by the occupation. It was quite understandable, this mood of the population because I am sure any occupation in the world is bad for the country. The farmers when we first met them...well, they said 'good morning' and we said 'good morning.' It was, anyway, difficult for the first month or should I say even the first two years to make really friendships. If you could speak a bit of English – also French because the farmers were speaking that dialect – you came in touch very quick with the population.

177

When the Germans began building concrete bunkers and observation towers Werner Grosskopf saw how the Islanders viewed these additions to the landscape.

> *Not only Jersey but Guernsey, Sark and Alderney were full of building machines and cement. It was horrible how many people from the Nazi Organisation Todt came over to build these bunkers. And the resentment – just of the farmers – was very sharp because, you must imagine, where these bunkers had been built we had taken away perhaps the best land of the farmer. And then, from the various campaigns, they brought over foreign workers and that was a great distress – to see these people living in barracks, getting small rations and working day and night to build these bunkers for us. And when one bunker was finished it often happened that three weeks later the pioneers had to blow it up because it was in the wrong place. And I was always saying to my soldiers there are too many cooks preparing the pie here.*

That the concrete constructions were a species of vandalism was an opinion held even more strongly by the local inhabitants, farmers or not, who saw their surroundings disfigured by these extensive defence works. Werner Grosskopf, like many soldiers of all ranks, believed that the fortifications were far too elaborate. He also thought that most people did not blame the Army for the orders of Hitler carried out by the Todt Organisation. Nor did he think that accusations of German brutality were true.

> *All citizens of St.Helier and also the farmers and the population in the countryside have found out, I would say, that the Germans are not like their newspapers and the radio have told them. They have seen that the Germans are a kind people. And the main thing, I think, is that they have seen that we have been very disciplined.*

178

Not far away, in the Alderney concentration camp, the routine treatment of prisoners included executions by hanging, flogging and beatings to the point of death. The methods of keeping discipline practised by the camp's SS personnel were described by a German prisoner who survived, Otto Spehr, originally from Hamburg. His crime was to distribute leaflets against Hitler and the Nazi regime for which he went first to prison, then to a series of concentration camps, finally arriving in Alderney. He was among a batch of a thousand prisoners in the transport. A large number of them found that at first there was no shelter in the camp for sleeping, as Otto Spehr remembered:

The first few days most of us had to spend the night in the open, there were only four or five buildings ready. We had to build the others. And so we lay outside where we could. Then later we had to build bunkers, fortifications and roads, lay cables and other such work, under the supervision of the SS.

Officially we were given the same rations by the commissariat as the armed forces because we were classed as manual labourers. But unfortunately we didn't get them because the SS asked for double helpings of breakfast for themselves and sold too much on the black market in Germany.

In the morning we got up at five o'clock, cleaned the barracks, had breakfast – those that had anything for breakfast. Then, next was the line up. We were counted to see whether we were all there. That usually took a while. And then we went to work at six – either six or seven o'clock, depending on the time of the year. There was a watery soup for lunch, a bit of cabbage or turnip in it or something else, a bit of bacon, a few potatoes. And when we got back in the evening, about six o'clock, there was a check again to see whether everything was there – all the tools. That always took hours. Then supper was given out. Everyone got a piece of bread – that is, one loaf was divided between six people. That had to do for the whole of the next day. And then there were ten grammes of margarine and sometimes a slice of sausage or a slice of cheese. At the end – something to drink that was called coffee.

Otto Spehr would one day return to his home town, Hamburg. To do so he had to survive in the camp and he knew that the best hope of survival lay in keeping out of trouble.

There were a lot of beatings and other hard treatment. For example, there was a man who moved a few steps from his place of work. This was reported to the camp commandant and he got twenty lashes with the horsewhip in the evening. And so for every little thing there was at least twenty, maybe twenty five. The Russians always said 'twenty-five holies.' There were beatings every day.

The SS people were very brutal. There was a Russian rummaging in the rubbish heap. He got some potato peel out for himself and was seen doing this by the SS. He was hit with the butt of a rifle. They smashed in the whole of his skull. Afterwards they called it 'accident. Skull fracture due to accident.'

There were a lot of hangings. They weren't hanged officially. They committed suicide – in the records. But in reality it was made sure that the other prisoners did the hanging – for which they got a reward. A lot died of malnutrition. The body got very weak. About thirty men were shot because they all had tuberculosis. And they just called it 'shot while escaping.' The camp fence was cut and they had to go out through a hole in the wire. Outside they were shot. Shot while escaping.

There were all kinds of people in the camp – all nations. Russians, Poles, Czechs. They were the main contingent. Then there were Frenchmen, Norwegians ... people were there from all the occupied countries. And all occupations, too – doctor or engineer to the ordinary worker. There were a thousand of us when we came. And when we left there were only about six hundred and fifty – I can't say the exact number.

To Alderney – but not to the concentration camp – came Major Paul

180

Markert with three hundred and sixty men. It was in the early days of the Occupation and his task was to organise defence and, clearly, as an Army man he had nothing to do with the SS. The Channel Islands seemed something of a novelty to him.

We were very surprised that we were pushed so far west but command is command and we followed orders. When we landed in Alderney we found a lot of destroyed cars, empty houses and, at first sight, no people. About eight days later a so-called Mr. Oselton turned up. He was staying in Alderney because he did not want to leave his cows. At that time he was about fifty years old – an honest, upright man, a very respectable man. He seemed to be a little sad because he had no cigarettes. On the other hand, we had enough and why shouldn't we have given him any? Sometimes he returned our favour by giving us some butter or fresh milk, and above all, he took me out fishing - for lobsters and general fishing. He knew the coast very well.

Life there was very boring for the men. But I took some precautions against this and, as I had several university graduates among them, I formed some study groups. For example, some were studying the science of industrial management or engineering while others were kept busy with medical studies and problems. And then I had a landscape gardener who started designing and laying out gardens.

One day he came to me and said: "There are these old casemates. They are always damp and tend to keep the same temperature – ideal for growing mushrooms." I said: "Where do you want to get the mushrooms from?" "Send me home on leave and I'll bring back enough spores," he said. And so I did. We sowed the mushrooms, added some horse manure and later on we had enough mushrooms to feed all of our three hundred and sixty men once a week. These jobs pleased the men and stopped them from being bored. According to my experience, if people have nothing to do they easily fall into doing some thing stupid.

181

Paul Markert received orders to go to Jersey where he was to take charge of two hundred recruits. He found Jersey more cheerful than Alderney. There were cinemas, cabarets and dances. The people there were approachable although a little reserved, he thought.

There was – how can I explain – not really a hostile atmosphere. We sort of respected each other. We tolerated each other and the situation we were in. There was a war on. What could we do? They didn't want it, we didn't want it. We don't really want to talk about who wanted it, do we?

I have to say that in Jersey there was a relatively good understanding. I remember once when I was driving from my regiment down to St. Helier - it was rather a steep road. On the right hand side there were some houses. All of a sudden a young child dashed out into the road. The only thing I could do was to pull my car around and against the kerbstone in order to avoid the little boy. The car was smashed - the shaft broken - but thank God the child escaped unhurt. The mother had seen the accident from a window. She came out, white as a sheet and trembling like a leaf. She thanked me again and again. I said it was all right – just my duty. One can replace a car but hit a child, no. He might have been killed.

Later, every time I drove past the house, they recognised the new car and they waved in a friendly way. People are like that. One has to be human, doesn't one?

Major Paul Markert did not seem to know much about the slave camps in Jersey but he did recall the prisoners in Alderney.

I only knew they were voluntary labourers from the East – Ukranians. Some time later I saw that they were existing under the most miserable conditions. Really you couldn't call that living. And there was a guard – a negro – who beat them up mercilessly. I then had the leader of the camp ordered to me and I told him that if this should ever happen again I would shoot the negro on the spot – and he should know that and act accordingly. So that was stopped as far as I know but many of the labourers died through malnutrition, weakness and exhaustion. Later it was discovered that much of their food was taken away and sent back to Germany. There was an inquiry and those responsible were removed. But I don't know what happened to them. Really, I haven't been in the camp at all. I only watched and saw that they were terribly beaten up. I did not agree with this. I took no part in it. As far as Alderney was concerned, I did know that there was this concentration camp but we didn't want to have anything to do with that.

What comes out in these personal reminiscences is the difference between the fantasies in Hitler's dreams of conquest and the outlook of the average German in the forces. One of the ex-soldiers went so far as to say: 'I am a pacifist. I am a good Catholic and always have a love for my fellow men.' And yet he was part of the military machine which dominated the Channel Islands between 1940 and 1945.

CHAPTER 18

Arguments and Conclusions

IN THE MIDDLE YEARS of the Occupation German officers and other ranks had to deal with the boredom which goes with a prolonged period of inaction. Some used the time to improve their knowledge of the English language. Others attended classes on useful subjects and there was one instance of an officer studying local wild flowers and plants.

Soldiers had, of course, military duties – parades, drills and the cleaning of weapons. But off duty hours allowed time for the pursuit of young women some of whom found the Germans an irresistible temptation. Ought they to have had such close encounters with the enemy? "'Why not?" one German is on record as saying. "After all, we were not cannibals." As time went by a number of healthy but illegitimate babies were born. In Guernsey those which could be ascribed to the Germans totalled 285 for the Occupation period, a hundred more than a similar maternity count in Jersey.

One venue where it was easy for soldiers to approach local girls was the beach. The Germans liked to go swimming and one of them said that the beach was ideal for breaking down barriers between the Army and the Islanders. "With everyone in bathing costumes, we were all the same."

Garrison talk about the progress of the war filled in part of the off-duty time, although opinions were not at first too rashly expressed for fear of reports by the Field Police. One soldier later said that he began to have doubts about an ultimate victory when Hitler sent the German Army to Russia. A war on two fronts must, he thought, end in disaster. The invasion of Normandy by the Allies was another moment when many realised that Germany would suffer defeat sooner or later. Rommel himself said that if the Allies could hold their bridgehead in Normandy for twenty four hours the German front in France would last no more than a few months. Then, in July, 1944, the bomb in the suitcase which nearly killed Hitler signalled that the end was in sight. Indications such as these showed a gradual deterioration in the morale of the troops.

Life in all its various permutations unfolded in the middle years and sometimes provided the Germans with unusual wartime experiences. Hans Glauber, a Navy petty officer, was in charge of a group of sailors in Sark where he and this team were erecting a battery of naval guns. Sark was always different from the other communities in Guernsey and Jersey and it continued to be exceptional through all the years of the Occupation. In its small area of 2.1 square miles a population of 471 sustained itself by farming and fishing. Hans Glauber remembered the time when he and his group of sailors first arrived:

> *Our first impression was that this was the end of the world. We hadn't ever seen a wilderness like Sark. We were wondering what we had let ourselves in for. Our official contact was with the Dame of Sark, a very severe person, not at all like somebody who should have been in charge of the island. We had always understood that anywhere connected with England was democracy. Then, to come here and find almost a dictatorship – that was quite a surprise. Her word was absolute law. Even us – we had to do more or less what she wanted.*
>
> *We had various arrangements with her. If we cut down timber and chopped it up for firewood she gave us some of it. She could speak German and one or two people in the Island could also speak a bit. They were already used to the Occupation when we arrived.*

The crisis period came in the last nine months of the war when Sark, like the other Islands, was short of food. Petty Officer Glauber said that rations were down to the barest minimum and had to be supplemented with whatever his men could find. In those nine months he lost 47 kilos in weight (about seven and a half stones).

Unless you've been really hungry, you cannot know what it's

*like. Your whole being thinks of nothing but where you can get
something to eat. We started on rabbits but soon we were
eating cats and dogs. I even shot two seagulls and there is a
superstition that in a seagull there is the soul of a dead sailor.
That's how desperate we were.*

*One day we caught a cat. First we cut the head off and
skinned it. Then we prepared it in a two gallon zinc bucket. We
had to boil it for about two hours in order to get rid of the bugs
which cats have. We added some nettles, a few potatoes and
some parsnips and made a sort of stew. Then it was put on a
beautiful white table-cloth with the proper knives and forks. It
was a real feast. There was one of us who had always said he
would never eat a cat or dog, although he would eat a rabbit.
After we'd finished I said to him – 'how did you like your
rabbit?' 'Wonderful,' he said. Then I told him – you've just
eaten a nice big tom-cat. He wouldn't believe it. 'Come off it,'
he said in his German way. Then we showed him the skin
When he saw it he went outside and brought it all back again.
Eating cats was cruel but that's the sort of thing you had to do
if you were going to stay alive.*

Earlier in 1944, before the Allied invasion of Normandy, food supplies
were still adequate. It was at that time that Lieutenant Hans Jurgen
Killmann disembarked in Jersey. He remembers his first months in the
island because of his meeting with Gretchen, the woman who quite soon
was to be his wife. She was a nurse in the *Soldatenheim* at the Mayfair Hotel
in St Helier. Her group of nurses had come over together and she could
remember their first impressions of Jersey.

*We were enraptured – the flowers, the daffodil fields and all
the pine trees and the climate – it had always been our dream
to come to the Channel Islands. There were about six or eight
of us and one supervisor in the soldiers' recreation home. Each
nurse had her own area which she was responsible for. We had
reading rooms, games rooms and we had a large visitors'*

room for social evenings and birthday celebrations.

Many soldiers came to the Soldatenheim *just in order to talk to us and tell us their worries. We always listened and tried to help. The supervisor made sure we behaved properly. Our work was subject to very strict moral laws but it was also possible for a soldier to fall in love with a nurse – and vice versa. You can see the best example of that in me and my husband. But that had to be kept a secret. Otherwise one partner was posted to another island.*

Her husband, Hans Jugen Killmann, had an additional reason for thinking he was lucky to have landed in Jersey.

I had some knowledge of English from school and we had an instructor who had studied at Oxford. He familiarised us thoroughly with the English situation. I knew therefore that I was coming to a people who are somehow related to us North Germans. It is well known that the Angles and Saxons went over to England in the year 450. And so we could assume that the way of the English was related and similar to ours. This is why we could only be pleased about coming to this front. We also knew that we would be treated correctly, even as prisoners - which was not the case on all the other fronts.

In the middle years of the Occupation German judges arrived in the Islands to preside over courts which were in addition to the Royal Courts of the Bailiffs and Jurats of the two bailiwicks of the Channel Islands. To Jersey came Judge Heinz Harmsen who, as it turned out, proved to have a liberal point of view which evidently stemmed from an era before Hitler.

On one occasion judge Harmsen had to examine the case of two boys who had stolen dynamite from an engineer's store of explosives. The boys had been searching for detonators when they were arrested. Judge Harmsen explained what happened:

It was their intention to blow up the States building as a protest against the supposed collaboration of the Island authorities. For this the boys had to be punished under the Young Persons Act. But it was a very difficult case. In my opinion the penalty for what they had done was death. But we just couldn't give that sentence. It was out of the question. Then we thought of the following way out.

In Germany we had the Juvenile Court Act – and that is what we applied in this case. It had to be proved that they had the necessary understanding at their age of what they wanted to do. I ruled that they were too stupid for that. So they were punished only on the count of theft.

And then I thought to myself – I don't want them to go in with the adults we had in prison. What could I do with them? I rang Sir Aubin (Charles Duret Aubin, Jersey's Attorney General). And we came to an understanding. He said: "I know a farmer in the north of the island and he has sometimes given a strict routine to boys like that. I suggest that they are taken to him and brought up by hard work." I agreed and the matter was settled.

That was the only case of sabotage which I experienced as a judge in the island. I must mention another case – not sabotage but serious anti-state activities. There were two sisters, Frenchwomen by birth, living in a house in St. Brelade's Bay. They were interested in art and it was in that house that I first saw paintings by Max Ernst. One of them could speak German. The other couldn't. They were arrested one day because it was discovered that they had been typing messages on cigarette papers and giving them to German troops. The messages said – Kill your officers. Put sand in your engines. Your war is lost. They were inciting the troops to undermine the loyalty of the armed forces and for this the penalty was death.

We had a big hearing before the court and of course the death sentence was given. But in every death sentence each of the judges must comment in a sealed envelope on the question

188

of mercy. I said to the defending counsel – a German officer who was a lawyer – that he should file a petition of mercy. And he said - why? It is right that they are being sentenced to death. I said – of course you must file a petition. I hereby give you an official order to file a petition for mercy.

The Bailiff also filed a petition. In it he maintained that for a hundred years no man had been executed in the Island, and for time immemorial no woman. And so files were packed up and a plane came from Germany and took them away. I hoped I would never see them again. The war would soon be over anyway. Just imagine: the files came back. I put them on the table and walked several times round before I dared open them. I found with great relief that they had been pardoned and given ten year's penal servitude - that would be in the island because we were isolated after the British and Americans went into Normandy.

Judge Harmsen was an accomplished amateur musician and in his spare time he joined other musical officers to play quartets, often going to a house where the acoustics were particularly good. Their host seemed pleased to let them use the room and this, the Judge thought, was an example of a friendly attitude which nevertheless did not go beyond what was correct behaviour in the circumstances.

Karl Heinz Kassens, an officer in the German Navy, said, "You found friendliness in every way from the inhabitants of Guernsey. But when we later came to Jersey it was not the same. There was a difference in the mentality of the two Islands."

Wilhelm Reiff, an NCO in an artillery regiment, said that when he first arrived in Jersey he found the people rather reserved. "They were very suspicious of us," he said. "We got the idea that they were saying – there go the Germans. They are bad. They are vile. But afterwards they saw that there was a certain human relationship between us."

At times it was difficult for Islanders to maintain an aloof attitude. Christian Schmidt, a private stationed in a country parish in Jersey, remembered a farmer asking him if he could bring some soldiers to help lift up a sick cow. After that Schmidt was always welcome at the farmhouse and offered cider from the farmer's private store.

Quite a number of Germans in the Islands seemed relieved when the news came through that Hitler was dead. One said "Good riddance." Another said that he knew this was the end and that the war was lost. Most of them were sure that they would be going to prisoner of war camps. A few hoped they would be able to go home. One said that he thought they would have to march from St. Malo all the way to Germany.

When they realised that their occupation of the Channel Islands would soon cease one member of the forces was in a special position to understand the overall situation. He was the Chief Naval Telecommunications Officer, Willi Hagedorn.

"At least a fortnight before the capitulation we were jammed on the radio by night. It was this big British station on the Isle of Wight. Finally we got a connection with them and I had orders to arrange a meeting point between the German and British forces. After the capitulation we carried on our wireless service for the British."

Willi Hagedorn remembered various contacts with Islanders and mentioned that he knew of certain people who had radio sets hidden in their houses. But he did not report them to the police. Most of the people he knew seemed reasonable and fair to him and he treated them in the same way.

"We had two housekeepers in our officers' mess, they were two Guernsey women. When the British liberation force was on its way to the Islands, I told them they had better stay away from us for their own sakes. And they said – no, you gave us food when we needed it. We shall carry on until the liberation is here."

Willi Hagedorn was another of the Germans who was glad to hear the news of Hitler's death

"We were elated by it. We thought – now it must be over in a few days. But in fact the war went on for three more weeks. Then we were all collected and marched down to the beach to get aboard the American liberty boats and then on to the big troopships for England.

Like thousands of others in the Islands he was destined for a prisoner of war camp.

"I must say," said Willi Hagedorn, "that during those days the civilians behaved in a deeply British way. They were very fair. I think it was the British mentality – the British character. They don't take things too seriously. They cope with the actual situation as it comes."

A similar comment on the British came from a German naval officer who was in a batch of prisoners taken aboard one of the Royal Navy ships.

"The officers of the British Navy," he said, "were markedly polite. At their head, the captain treated us with exquisite courtesy and his officers let us know that they regretted seeing us in this situation."

German attitudes were not always the same because temperaments varied in the different regions. It is a country not of one people but of many. There were the Prussians, aristocratic and military minded, the North Germans, stubborn and hard working, the Rhinelanders, easy going and pleasure loving and the Bavarians, good humoured and convivial. Nevertheless, in their times of national crisis they joined in supporting a German point of view on the world around them, as expressed in their word *Weltanschauung* which included a belief in the superior status of Germany over the comity of nations and a militant will to power.

Three times in less than a century the Germans have made war on their European neighbours, ruining the stable conditions of nearly a dozen sovereign nations - in 1870, in 1914 and again in 1939. Bismarck's dream of a German hegemony started an expansion beyond regional borders and carried over into the ambitions of Kaiser Wilhelm and the men of 1914. Politicians and soldiers at the time joined in the patriotic anthem. *Deutschland Uber Alles* – I believe above all in Germany.

With the declaration of war in 1914 the British Foreign Secretary, Sir Edward Grey, uttered his prophetic words: "The lamps are going out all over Europe. We shall not see them lit again in our lifetime." The chaos inside Germany following the collapse of 1918 led to the rise of Hitler and the take-over of all German institutions by the Nazi Party. The ill-conceived Versailles Treaty of 1919 had destroyed the Austro-Hungarian Empire and left a vast area of central Europe ripe for conquest by a resurrected German Army. It was a vacuum waiting to be filled. Hitler first imposed his regime on Czechoslovakia and Austria by internal subversion but then he was ready, in 1939, to invade Poland. The era of the *blitzkrieg* had begun.

Ordinary Germans, hypnotised all over again by promises of a glorious future, began the war believing in the cause of Greater Germany and enjoying the first easy victories. But on the battlefields of Russia and in the west they lost their innocence. Those who later saw what had happened were overcome by a sort of grief. Werner Grosskopf, one time NCO stationed in Jersey, remembered the news coming through of the Normandy invasion and later of the battles which followed.

"It was terrible for me - and all the soldiers around me - to see how our boys and the American boys and your boys were killed on this devilish invasion front in Normandy and in Belgium and Germany."

An echo of this sentiment emerged after the war in a German song which everyone heard on the radio at the time – *Sag mir wo die Blumen sind.* The words expressed a nostalgia and heartache for the years of sacrifice. "Where have all the flowers gone? Long long ago the girls gave them to their young men. And where have all the young men gone? Gone to be soldiers, every one. So tell me where the flowers are. *Sag mir wo die Blumen sind.* They are growing on the soldiers' graves." It was the lament of a generation.

In the nineteen forties those Germans who came to the Channel Islands, staying for a while, were thus spared the massacres of the continental war fronts. Their testimonies and observations on day to day living show how it felt to be stationed among a people whose lives had been overwhelmed by the upheavals of the Second World War.

Few events could have seemed more shocking and disastrous than the sudden appearance of the Germans in Jersey, Guernsey and Sark. And yet by the end of the war something had changed. Aside from the anger and fear of those in the deportations or in the custody of the police, a mutual understanding, only half realised, began to reduce the differences between soldier and civilian. It showed itself in small ways. At the time of the Liberation some Jersey people came to say goodbye to a German officer. They said with some embarrassment: "You must understand that we are glad to have the Tommies back here." And he replied as he was led away to captivity, "that's all right."

Looking back on the War and the Occupation a question comes up again and again. How was it possible that so many people could be pressed into service to make war against the countries of Europe. Is there something in the history of the Germans going back to Attilla the Hun which accounts for their ambitions? Some commentators have noted that the Roman Empire stopped at the Rhine and consequently its civilising influence did not reach the territories of the barbarians.

A more likely explanation is that the Germans, like the Dutch, the French and the British, were in the forefront of Europe's industrial and commercial expansion of the nineteenth and twentieth centuries. Rivalry in the search for raw materials, markets and spheres of influence powered a relentless drive to achieve dominion and wealth and the Germans did not have a balanced political system to contain it. The great majority of people had to follow the lead of whoever gained control of the central government. Those who saw what was happening and objected soon disappeared into prisons and concentration camps.

That the enigma of Germany lies in pressures from international politics is what many people believe to be the reason for the eruptions of the past which culminated in the two world wars. Historical influences continuously shift over the years from one national movement to another until suddenly circumstances arise when, like the opening of a strong room door by turning a code sequence in the lock, the counters click into place and war is inevitable.

The effect on people living in the areas of conflict leaves them with the imperative of meeting the challenge in one way or another and of seeking a new adjustment to the situation. When men and women in the Channel Islands think back to the occupation their memories linger first on the outward forms imposed by the German Military Government with all its regulations, inconveniences and, in the case of the police, its brutality. They also remember exceptions in the system, as shown by individual members of the armed forces whom they encountered in the course of everyday life.

Those Germans who returned as tourists in later years found that, on the whole, the Islanders accepted them as being the same as any other group of visitors. But people whose relatives or friends had died in the prisons or concentration camps of the Nazi regime could not bring themselves to forgive. For them only a lifetime could heal their bitterness. Another generation would have to come and go before memories could be dimmed and the past forgotten. Experiences varied, some more intense, others less so. The Occupation was like an immense pageant and people played different parts in the drama.

With the present movement towards a union of European nations it seems unlikely that the differences between those who endured the Occupation and the Germans who found themselves in the Islands as Occupiers will ever again be so sharply contrasted nor is it conceivable that the Channel Islands will suffer invasion by any other foreign army. The age old fear of the French and latterly of the Germans which has haunted the minds of Jerseymen and Guernseymen for centuries must at last fade away in the new alignments of the Europe of the future.

BIBLIOGRAPHY

PUBLICATIONS:

The German Occupation of the Channel Islands – Official History: Charles Cruikshank, Oxford University Press, 1975.
Memoirs of Lord Coutanche; Compiled by Tom Pocock, Phillimore, 1975.
German Armour in the Channel Islands: Channels Islands Occupation Society.
Jersey Under the Jackboot: R.C.F. Maugham, W.H. Allen, 1946.
One Man's War: Frank Stroobant, Burbridge, Guernsey, 1967.
The German Occupation of Jersey: Leslie Sinel, La Haule Books, 1985.
Chronicle of the 20th Century: Edited by Derick Mercer, Longmans, 1988.
Second World War: Martin Gilbert, Weidenfeld & Nicholson, 1989.
Islands in Danger: Alan and Mary Seton Wood, Evans Brothers, 1955.
German Fortifications in Jersey: Michael Ginns and Peter Bryans, Meadowbank, Jersey, 1975.
Channel Islands Occupation Review: Edited by Matthew Costard, Channel Islands Occupation Society.
Hitler's Fortress Islands: Carel Toms, Hodder & Stoughton, 1978.
Channel Islands Occupied: Richard Mayne, Jarrold, 1985.
A Doctor's Occupation: John Lewis, Corgi Books, 1982.
The Silent War: Frank Falla, Frewin, 1967.
Jersey Occupation Remembered: Sonia Hillsdon, Jarrold, 1986.
Jersey under the Swastika: Ralph Mollet, Hyperion Press, 1945.
Swastika over Guernsey: Victor Coysh, Guernsey Press, 1974.
The Dame of Sark: Sybil Hathaway, Heinemann, 1961.
The von Aufsess Occupation Diary: Baron von Aufsess, Phillimore, 1985.

OTHER SOURCES:

Imperial War Museum Archives.
Library of Impact Video Productions.
Priaulx Library, Guernsey.
Library of Channel Television.
Jersey Archives Service.
Bundesarchiv, Freiberg, Germany.

The Fuhrer and Supreme Commander of the Forces,
Fuhrer's Headquarters.

20.10.41

Fortification and Defence of the English Channel Islands

1.   English operations on a large scale against the territories occupied by us in the West are, now as before, unlikely. But under pressure of the situation in the East, and for reasons of politics and propaganda, small scale operations must at any moment be reckoned with, particularly an attempt to regain possession of the Channel Islands, which are important to us for the protection of our sea communications.

2.   Counter-measures in the Channel Islands must ensure that any English attack fails before a landing is effected, whether it be attempted by sea or air or by both simultaneously. The possibility of the enemy taking advantage of bad visibility to make a surprise landing must be borne in mind.   Emergency measures for strengthening the defences have already been ordered. All branches of the Forces stationed in the Islands are placed under the orders of the Commandant of the Islands, except the Air Force.

3.   With regard to the permanent fortifying of the Islands to convert them into an impregnable fortress (which must be pressed forward at maximum speed) I give the following orders:-

(a)   The High Command of the Army is responsible for the fortifications as a whole and will incorporate in the overall programme the constructions needed for the Navy and Air Force.   The strength of the fortifications and the order in which they are built will be based on the principles and practical knowledge derived from the building of the Western Wall.

(b)   For the Army it is urgent to provide:- A close network of emplacements, as far as possible with flanking fire, which must be well concealed (sufficient for guns of the size required to pierce 100 mm. armour plate) for defence against tanks which may be landed from flat-bottomed boats; accommodation for mobile diversion parties and armoured cars;
accommodation for ample stores of ammunition, including that for the Navy and Air Force; incorporation of mine-fields into the defence system.

The total number of buildings estimated as necessary must be reported.

(c)   The Navy has for the safeguarding of the sea approaches 3 batteries of the heaviest type, one in Guernsey and two on the French coast; and furthemore it will eventually have with the help of the Army

Appendix 1 on pages 198 and 199: Hitler's orders for the fortification of the Islands (English translation).

This document came into the possession of La Société Guernesiaise, given to the Society by His Excellency the Lieutenant-Governor of Guernsey, translations being made from the German by The Reverend A. Bourde de la Rogerie and Miss Kathleen Nowlan who then agreed a final draft.

By courtesy of the Priaulx Library, Guernsey.

The Fuhrer and Supreme Commander of the Forces,
Fuhrer's Headquarters.

20.10.41

Fortification and Defence of the English
Channel Islands

1.   English operations on a large scale against the
territories occupied by us in the West are, now as before, unlikely.
But under pressure of the situation in the East, and for reasons
of politics and propaganda, small scale operations must at any
moment be reckoned with, particularly an attempt to regain
possession of the Channel Islands, which are important to us for
the protection of our sea communications.

2.   Counter-measures in the Channel Islands must ensure
that any English attack fails before a landing is effected,
whether it be attempted by sea or air or by both simultaneously.
The possibility of the enemy taking advantage of bad visibility
to make a surprise landing must be borne in mind.   Emergency
measures for strengthening the defences have already been ordered.
All branches of the Forces stationed in the Islands are placed
under the orders of the Commandant of the Islands, except the Air
Force.

3.   With regard to the permanent fortifying of the Islands
to convert them into an impregnable fortress (which must be pressed
forward at maximum speed) I give the following orders.=

(a)   The High Command of the Army is responsible for
       the fortifications as a whole and will incorporate
       in the overall programme the constructions needed
       for the Navy and Air Force.   The strength of the
       fortifications and the order in which they are
       built will be based on the principles and practical
       knowledge derived from the building of the Western
       Wall.

(b)   For the Army it is urgent to provide:- A close
       network of emplacements, as far as possible with
       flanking fire, which must be well concealed
       (sufficient for guns of the size required to
       pierce 100 mm. armour plate) for defence against
       tanks which may be landed from flat-bottomed
       boats; accommodation for mobile diversion parties
       and armoured cars;
       accommodation for ample stores of ammunition,
       including that for the Navy and Air Force;
       incorporation of mine-fields into the defence
       system.

       The total number of buildings estimated as necessary
       must be reported.

(c)   The Navy has for the safeguarding of the sea
       approaches 3 batteries of the heaviest type, one in
       Guernsey and two on the French coast; and furthemore
       it will eventually have with the help of the Army

light and medium coastal batteries on the islands
themselves and on the French coast suitable for
firing on targets at sea, so that the whole Bay
may be protected.

(d) For the Air Force strong points must be created
with searchlights sufficient to accommodate
such Anti-Aircraft Units as are needed for the
protection of all important constructions.

(e) Foreign labour, especially Russian and Spanish
but also French, may be used for the building
operations.

4. Another order will follow for the deportation to the
Continent of all Englishmen who are not native Islanders,
i.e. who were not born in the Islands.

5. The progress of the fortifications must be reported to me
on the 1st of each month through the Com.-in Chf., Army,
directed to the Supreme Command of the Armed Forces,
Staff of the Fuhrer, Division L.

(Signed) A.H. (i.e. Adolf Hitler)

General geographical and tactical data

on the

F o r t r e s s e s

G u e r n s e y , J e r s e y and A l d e r n e y

- as at 1.9.44 -

The British Channel Islands shut off the northern portion of the deeply penetrating, right angled bay of St Malo, which is formed by the Cotentin and Brittany peninsulas.

A. Geographical

1. Situation

        (Note by translator. See map. Translation
        of writing on map)   "Situation of the islands
        relative to England and France."
        Scale 1 : 2,500,000

MAP

2. Size:

	Guernsey	Sark	Jersey	Alderney	Total
Area	66	7	116	8	197 sq. km.
Length of coastline	52	15	84	17	148 km.

Each of the 11 batallions stationed on the three islands is allocated 13 kilometres of coastline.

Appendix 2: Geographical and Tactical Data (English version).

200

Strongpoint Hommet

1. **Sector** between the strongponts Picquerel Point and La Pequerie.

2. ..**Strength:** Own   3 N.C.Cs   18 men.

                Attached (searchlight crew)   2 men..

3. **Armanent:** Own: 1 105 mm casemate gun (f), fortress type
   1 50 mm anti-tank gun.
   1 37 mm anti-tank gun (f) in armoured cupola.
   2 light machine guns 34.
   2 machine guns 311(f) in armoured cupola.
   1 80 mm grenade thrower.
   1 50 mm grenade thrower.
   Attached: 1 60 cm anti-aircraft searchlight.

4. **Battle Task:** The strongpoint Hommet has the task to repel any landing attempt by sea or air, in its allocatec sector. The sector of the strongpoint is in the south west part of Grand Havre, Rousse peninsular as well as the westward lying Bay of Port Grat.

5. **Battle Instructions:** The strongpoint Hommet lies south of the Rousse peninsular on the road to Red 2. It is bounded on the sides by two roads that lead to road Red 2. The casemate gun covers Grand Havre and engages any landing on the shore. One machine gun 311(f) covers the shore to the east of Rousse. The 50 mm and 37 mm anti-tank guns, in armoured cupolas, have above all the task to engage enemy armour, which may attempt to break in from the Bay of Port Grat, or out of the west along Road 2 into the area between Strongpoint Hommet and the Quarry Battery. The two machine guns cover the same space. The 80 mm and 50 mm grenade throwers supplement the fire of the other weapons and cover areas which are not accessible to level fire.

   The Quarry Battery will support the defensive fire in the space to the westward of the strongpoint with the two 20 mm anti-aircraft guns, one 76.2 mm anti-tank guns(r) and one 37 mm anti-tank gun in armoured cupola. One machine gun 311(f) and one light machine gun 34 are provided for rearward efence.

   In tne event of an attack from the landward side, a storm troop of the strongpoint will man intermediate field positions.

Appendix 3: Instructions from OKW Berlin on the manning and operation of Strong-Point Hommet in Guernsey (English version).

STRONG POINT (LARGE) FORT HOMMET

1. <u>Sector</u> between strong points Lion Rock and Martello Tower No. 12.

2. <u>Strength:</u>

Own:	4 N.C.Os.	30 men.
Attached:		
Searchlight crews (Army)	1 N.C.O.	4 men.
Searchlight crews (Navy Mirus Battery)	1 N.C.O.	5 men.
Georgiers of 2nd batallion		6 men.
	6 N.C.Os.	45 men.

3. <u>Armament:</u> Four heavy and two light machine guns.
   One 47 mm anti-tank gun.
   One machine gune 19.
   Four 105 mm casement guns.
   One light machine gun in armoured cupola.
   One medium and four defensive flame throwers.
   Two rifle grenade throwers.
   Two 60 cm and one 150 cm searchlights.
   Two Verey pistols.
   Four machine pistols (Tommy Guns).
   Six pistols.
   43 Rifles.
   One Abshussrohr (Rocket projector)

4. <u>Battle Task:</u> The Strong Fort Hommet has the duty:
   (a) to discover in good time any landing attempt
   in Cobo and Albecq Bays and, particularlarly in
   Vazon Bay, by constant observation of the sea and
   air.

   (b) In collaboration with the strong points of
   Cobo, Albecq and Vazon Bays, to defend the above
   places against any landing from the sea.

   (c) To defend Point Hommet and the strong point
   itself to the last man against any attck from
   the sea or land.

   (d) To support the neighbouring strong points.

   The main front line is the level of the coast line
   at high water.

5. Battle Instructions:

(a) The strong Point is to be constantly manned. Look-outs
are to be posted by day and night and, by day, the
anti-aircraft machine guns are to be manned. The coast
up to strong point Cobo Rock will be watched by the
provision of a patrol of 1 / 5 (This probably means
an N.C.O. and five men - Translator).

(b) Because of its commanding position on the headland, the
strong point blocks the entrance into Cobo and Albecq
Bays and, in particular, the entrance to Vazon Bay.
Every weapon is allotted its main line of fire, barrage
fire area and targets.
Weapons (apart from side arms) are to be constantly ready in
their firing positions. Sentries are to be placed at
the most important weapons. The gun crews will have their
sleeping quarters in the immediate vicinity.
As required, the strong point will order preparatory fire
from the artillery and A.A. guns in Cobo and Vazon Bays
and also lay on "Barrage Fire Vazon Bay."

(c) An enemy attack on Point Hommet may be expected from all
sides and, in particular, from the land. The strong
point is therefore built to withstand a concentric
attack. The peripheral defences will be manned when
the situation is not clear, as well as by night and in
foggy weather. The strong point is protected by mine
fields on the land side. Provison is made for bringing
into action close range anti-tank troops, as well as the
laying of a quick barrier with 'T' (Teller) mines in the
main mine field lanes. The defence cam be supported by
the strong points Lion Rock, Martello Tower No. 12 and
the Grenade throwing Battery Kings Mills.

(d) Strong Point Fort Hommet can give supporting fire to the
neighbouring strong points Lion Rock and Martello Tower
No. 12 in their near defence.
All available forces will be used for a counter-blow in
the defence of their own sector and in supporting the
neighbouring strong points.

Appendix 4: Strong-Point (large) Fort Hommet.
The fortification and manning of the strong-point envisaged as a wide arc
of defence on the west coast of Guernsey in the bays of Vazon, Cobo and
Albecq (English version).

INDEX

AAC BOOKS
BY POST
Channel Islands

ABOUT US

Visit our site /aacbooks.co.uk

AAC BOOKS BY POST is the mail order department of **Starlight Imports** and **Starlight Publishing**.

We are a Channel Islands based Wholesaler/Publisher who have supplied books to both the trade and mail order customers all over the world for the past 15 years.

Like many other businesses we are just starting to explore the potential of the worldwide web and this is our first site which will be growing constantly. So if you don't find anything of interest **please call again**.

Our aim is to send goods from us to you by post with the minimum of effort, so please feel free to CONTACT us if you have any queries.

TEL (01534) 860806
FAX (01534) 860811
E-mail: sales@aacbooks.co.uk

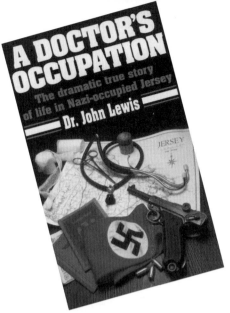

A DOCTOR'S OCCUPATION

In 1939 Dr. John Lewis was building up a successful general practice in Jersey.
In 1940, as the Germans were poised to invade the Channel Islands, he managed to get his pregnant wife safely across to England. He then returned to Jersey to look after his patients.

In 1945 the German garrison surrendered to the British. Five years of Occupation were at an end.

This is the story of Dr. Lewis's experiences during those years: a first-hand account of life in the only British territory to be controlled by Nazi Germany during World War II.   240 PAGES

Please send me ...... copies of *A Doctor's Occupation* @ £5.95 (£4.95 + £1.00 P&P)
I enclose a cheque / P.O. for .... made out to Starlight Publishing.

Name _____

Address _____

_____

_____

Starlight Publishing.Unit 3B Barette Commercial Centre,
La Route du Mont Mado   St John, Jersey JE3 4DS.
Tel (01534) 860806

Visit our Website, www.aacbooks.co.uk